Book It!

How to Write and Publish Your Business Authority Book, Without Going Crazy, So That You Can Get More Speaking Gigs, Get Media Attention, Attract Better Clients, and Make More Money!

By Sandi Masori

Sandi Masori

ISBN 13: 9781717823113

TABLE OF CONTENTS

ACKNOWLEDGMENTS

First, as always, I need to thank my family for putting up with my long hours writing this book. So here's a shout out to my children who allow me to work on the book when they would like me to pay attention to them; my mom for babysitting and cooking for my kids when I'm too wrapped up in the book to come up for air, and my dad for editing it.

Then I need to thank the authors who so generously gave of their time and allowed me to interview them for the book. I literally couldn't have done it without you.

Thank you to my BFF Ami for hosting me while I was in the final days of writing and just needed to sequester myself from the world.

Thank you to my mentors, Mike Keonigs and Ed Rush, for teaching me so much of what I know and being there to support me.

Thank you to Rachel Porter and Don Harrison, my "first responders" who read my book before it was done to see if I was on the right track.

Thank you to all of my clients for helping me become an expert in this by trial and error.

Thank you to my incredible team of editors, graphic designers and formatters for making this and my other clients' books look great.

And especially, thank you to you, the reader for giving me a reason to write.

HOW TO USE THIS BOOK

This book is meant to both inform and inspire you. The first part of this book is the "How To." This can be read all at once, or by topic. For example, are you most worried about where to publish? Then go straight to the Where to Publish section. Need to know about formatting? Then go to the Formatting section. Having trouble getting past the blank page? Go to the get it out of your head and onto paper section. Should you do a pre-release? There's a section for that too. Then we'll talk about what to do with your book once it's published.

Once we get past the technical stuff, I've interviewed some of my most inspiring clients so you can see how they got past the overwhelm, got their book done and what they got from publishing their book, (and becoming a best-selling author), and the advice they have for someone who is still thinking about writing the book, but hasn't done it yet.

You're free to read it cover to cover, or in small bites. Whatever works for you.

Everything you need to know is here in the book, but if you need more help writing, publishing, formatting, or launching it to best seller, come by my site and schedule an appointment with me and we'll see if and how I can help you expedite the process to make your dream of becoming a best-selling author a reality.

http://www.ExpertBook4U.com

MY STORY

I don't think anyone is more surprised than I that not only am I writing a book but it's my *seventh* bestselling book.

It all started when, in an effort to promote my balloon company, Balloon Utopia, I started attending marketing classes. I think the first one was in 2008 or 2009. Anyway, I began applying the things I was learning to Balloon Utopia, and to my surprise, they worked! In 2012, I was at a conference and the speaker casually mentioned writing a business authority book and making it a best-seller.

He said that he had dictated his book into his phone, focusing on the most frequently asked questions about his industry, and on the questions that he wished his customers would ask.

I thought to myself that I could do that. Then I realized that through the marketing classes I had been taking, I had already had a lot of the content written as I had made videos about those very topics. It's a format that one of my marketing mentors, Mike Keonigs, has been advocating for years, called the "10 x 10"- that is the 10 most frequently asked questions and the 10 should ask questions (FAQs and SAQs).

So, I took the videos and had them transcribed. Then I printed them out and literally cut and pasted them together. Next, I determined what information was missing and filled the holes. I thought about what other info would be useful for my target readers, who in that particular case were trade show organizers and exhibitors. Once I identified what else my readers needed to know, I wrote those chapters.

I had a huge pile of papers, which I transcribed to the computer. Yeah, I'm old school that way. In fact, at the time of this writing, I'm sitting here, early in the morning, on my vacation, and I'm writing this with pen and paper, and I'll transcribe it later.

Back to that first book: After I finished writing everything I reached out to a bunch of friends and asked them to edit/ proofread it for me. I also sent it to the best editor I've ever known, my dad, a lifelong journalist and editor, Don Harrison. (Yes, they are one and the same).

Honestly, the editing process ended up taking longer and being harder than the writing did.

After that was done, I had to figure out how to format it. Amazon has made self-publishing so accessible. It has a ton of info on how to format, so I painstakingly taught myself what to do. That part definitely led to some head banging.

But, I prevailed, and finally my first book, *The Ultimate Guide to Inflating Your TradeShow Profits …* was born.

It was exciting when the Kindle version of the title hit best-seller, but what made it real for me was when I was holding the physical book in my hands. My name was on the front cover and the spine. My bio along with an ISBN was on the back cover I really can't even express how emotional it was to hold it in my hands for the first time. I realized that, holy sh**, I was an author!! I had done it! It was a really emotional moment for me, second only to the birth of my two children.

In many ways, birthing a book is much like having a baby. And just like having a baby, you forget the labor pains. The next year, having forgotten the hair-tearing part, I did it again, and again, and again--the books, that is, not the babies! Which brings us to now, at the time of this writing, with me sitting in an empty restaurant on a cruise ship, trying to finish my seventh book. If you are reading this, then I succeeded. ;-)

The real question is what did I get from writing a book? Did I make millions and millions of dollars in book sales? No, I didn't. Unlike the movie, just because you build it does not mean that they will come. The magic is in what you do with it and how you leverage it.

I took that book and I sent it to planners and others who were in my target demographic. I arranged a meeting with the sales people at the convention center and gave a box of my books to them to give away.

Balloons have a bit of a stigma in that people tend to think that they're just for kids, or something to throw in at the last minute, and that all balloon people are clowns. By writing and publishing a book, I changed that perspective. When I gave my book to the convention center people they were blown away. The way they looked at me literally changed before my eyes. My status instantly went up, as did my credibility. I was obviously the biggest expert and authority on using balloons for trade shows because I literally had written the book on it.

Calls started coming for higher-ticket balloon sculptures. Some of the clients were of a higher dollar bracket than before. I got some media training and was invited to do media interviews throughout the nation, including on *The Today Show* and multiple appearances on the Hallmark Channel's *Home and Family Show*.

Writing a book changed the conversation and ultimately changed my life.

At the time of this writing, plans are being finalized for the sale of Balloon Utopia. I never imagined that I would be a serial entrepreneur and sell a business that I spent over 20 years building, and thought that I would do forever, but here I am, gleefully turning over the reins to one of my mentees and moving on to focus on what was for many years my professional hobby.

You see, after I published my first book, other people started to ask me to help them with theirs. To date, I've helped over 100 other experts, entrepreneurs, speakers and coaches to write and publish their books.

So, that's how it happens that I'm sitting here and marveling at the stroke of fate that has me making my hobby my full time gig, and what was my bread and butter (balloons, that is) will become my hobby.

Here's the crazy truth of it, once you write a book and put your effort behind promoting it, or using it as a piece of your marketing arsenal, you have no idea where it's going to take you, but I can definitely tell you it can be well beyond what you can even imagine. And if you need some help along the way, well, I'm here for you.

WHAT IS A BUSINESS AUTHORITY BOOK?

A business authority book is one that is written to provide people with information about your industry and to establish you as the "go to" expert in your field. Though your book probably will sell, it's more valuable as a marketing tool to leverage. Your focus should be more on making money WITH the book than on making money ON the book.

Besides establishing you as the expert, it's also a great way for you to train your customers/ clients, or patients.

Questions that you get asked over and over; procedures you have to explain again and again, all of those should be in your book. Instead of verbally explaining it yet again, you can gift a copy of your book to your clients and let them read it for themselves. They'll come to you as a more prepared, better informed clients.

TO SELF-PUBLISH OR NOT TO SELF-PUBLISH?

The biggest difference in self-publishing vs. traditional or hybrid publishing is the amount of control that you have over your book and how much marketing you have to do for it.

Of course, the dream for everyone is to be picked up by a traditional publisher, get paid a hefty advance and become the next Dr. Oz or Tony Robbins.

That's not quite the reality though. First of all, if your book was even accepted by a traditional publisher, it would take more than a year for it to actually come to market. Also, the publisher has all the control and may make a lot of changes to the book and the content. You may not have any say over the cover design or the general layout. Your royalties will be much much smaller, and your price to purchase individual copies much higher. But, if they are going to do all the marketing of it for you, it still might be a good way to go.

More often than not, authors fall into the clutches of the hybrid publishers. To this I say, Run away, run far far away!!

What is a hybrid publisher? Well, it's like self-publishing, but it goes under someone else's label, and they're going to charge you to publish your book, take over control of it, also control the rights to the book, control the pricing of the book, possibly lock you into a publishing contract for future books, still put the burden of marketing on you, and charge you a lot more for your author copies, which you may need to order 1,000 at a time. What do you get for all this? MAYBE your book will get carried in some of the smaller brick and mortar stores, maybe. As you can tell, I'm not a fan of the hybrid publishers.

And then there's self-publishing. Obviously, since this book is self- published that's my favorite, and here's why: with self-publishing you have all the control, all the rights, and can get it to market faster and on your own schedule. You can make changes whenever you want and the author copies are fairly inexpensive. As an added bonus, when you publish through KDP or Createspace, these author copies are the same price whether you buy 1 or 1000. There's no need to have a garage full of books collecting dust. And, if your book is a runaway success, those high end traditional publishers will seek you out with a much sweeter deal than if you tried to approach them.

WHERE TO PUBLISH YOUR BOOK

At the time of this writing there are three main places that people go to self-publish. Two of them are owned by Amazon. There are some subtle differences among the three.

Createspace and KDP are both under the Amazon umbrella. Createspace can publish the paperback, KDP can publish the kindle version and the paperback. The third option is Ingramspark, and it can publish the paperback and the hardback.

Let's first compare the two Amazon properties, which are what I use most often for my clients. First of all, the back end for both Createspace and KDP is the same – that is they use the same print houses. That means that there is no difference in quality between the end products of the two. Both require a PDF file for publishing the paperback. Both offer you the opportunity to buy your book at a discounted rate, and allow you to have that rate whether you're ordering one copy or 1,000 copies. Both KDP and Createspace will offer you a free ISBN.

The main difference at this point has to do with intent. What are you planning to do with your book? Are you planning to give it away or hope that people buy it? It may seem like a silly question; of course you hope that people will buy it, right? But here's what I mean, if your goal is to get speaking gigs or get your foot in the door somewhere, or train your clients, you may want to give the book directly to those prospects. If on the other hand, you are teaching something, as I do in my *DIY Balloon Bibles*, then you probably are more concerned with distribution and sales.

Createspace offers "expanded distribution." This means that the book is sent to other online retailers, including Barnes and Noble. Com, libraries and other online book sellers. They may not bring it into the brick and mortar store, which I'll explain in a minute, but generally they will offer it on their websites.

At the time of writing, KDP just started offering expanded distribution in the US, but it remains to be seen if it's as comprehensive as Createspace or not. The advantage of publishing through KDP is that they use the Amazon payment gateway, so you can order copies of your book at your special author price and then have Amazon send it as a gift to your prospects, clients, or patients. It's a great foot-in-the-door strategy to get past the gatekeeper.

Another difference is that KDP is faster at approving the books and doesn't pull down the content when making changes the way that Createspace does. This means that the old content will stay active until the new content has been approved. Createspace will pull it down, which means that you could have a short period of time where the book is not available for purchase.

My previous 6 books were published through Createspace. The first few I did through Createspace because that was the only option at the time, and the later ones I did there because I wanted the expanded distribution. This book, on the other hand, I'm publishing through KDP because I want the freedom to make changes quickly and to be able to send gift copies to clients and prospects.

Ingramspark is different in that you will need to supply your own ISBN, which you can buy through Bowker, and it offers expanded distribution to brick and mortar booksellers as well. It also offers hardback printing.

I have one client who is publishing his book through all three- we're doing the ebook through KDP, as Kindle is the 10,000 lb gorilla there; the paperback through Createspace as we want the discounted author copies and the expanded distribution Createspace offers' and the hardback through Ingram, as it was really important to him to have a hardback edition.

Ingramspark is a bit more complicated and really is most useful if you are moving from being a self-published author to being a publisher.

Let's put it this way, for all of the 100+ books I've helped publish, only one, the one mentioned above, needed to go through Ingramspark instead of staying with the Amazon properties.

12

The one place where it might really make a difference is if you are trying to get your book carried in brick and mortar bookstores. The physical bookstores rarely order self-published books because most self-publishing is done as "print on demand." What this means is that they don't print the book until it's ordered, and it's not really returnable.

Usually the brick and mortar stores will order a quantity of a book, and if it doesn't sell, they can send back the cover and get a refund on the unsold copies. KDP and Createspace do not allow for this option, so the bookstores will only get the book in by customer request. Ingramspark does offer this option, but you, as the publisher, bear the expense of the refund. Also, just because it's returnable does not mean that they will carry it- that would really depend on your marketing efforts.

THE COVER

They say that you shouldn't judge a book by the cover, but in this digital age, let's face it, not only are you being judged by the cover, you're being judged by the thumbnail of the cover. For that reason, it's really important that your cover shows up well as a thumbnail.

That means don't have too much text on it or too many complicated elements.

You should definitely hire a professional to help you here. If you don't really know what you want, 99 Designs is a great resource as you can create a contest and put it out to bid and different designers will submit ideas to you. If you already have an idea of what you want, or have some other books to use for inspiration, it will be even easier.

Here are a couple of other resources for you; Canva.com where you can use a template to design the cover on your own, Fiverr.com where you can hire freelancers for multiples of $5 and Upworks.com which is a freelance marketplace.

For my books, often I'll create a very bad mockup of my cover in Canva or Photoshop and then give it to my designer to make pretty.

For the Kindle edition, the cover should be 1000 x 1600 pixels, and output as a Jpeg. For the paperback the full cover size will depend on the number of pages as that will determine the width of the spine. The most common trim size though is 6 x 9. The file should be output as a high resolution PDF.

The back cover of the paperback is really important as well. It is my opinion that the back cover should have the book description on it. It's also nice to have the author's photo and a short bio. And, of course, be sure that you leave room for the ISBN (the book's bar code).

HOW LONG SHOULD IT BE?

I get asked this question a lot. My answer is always "as long as it needs to be to convey the information and no longer."

For Kindle it doesn't really matter, as there are no "pages" in the traditional sense. For the paperback on the other hand, it should be at least 120 pages or so (6x9 pages, so around 80 pages in word). The reason that this number is so important is that if the page count is less than that, the spine will not be wide enough to print on, and if you can't print on the spine, IMHO, you have a booklet, not a book. It's really important, because without the spine printing, it's hard to find on a bookshelf or in a stack of books.

There are some tricks we can do to fluff out a short book and make it longer if we need to add to the page count. Chapters generally start on the right side of the book, images can be full size and you can include some lined pages for notes.

Shortening a long book, on the other hand, is a job for an experienced high level editor. As Tolstoy reportedly said, the reason that *War and Peace* was so long was that he didn't have time to make it shorter.

WRITING YOUR BOOK

think this is the thing that overwhelms people more than anything else. How to get the seed of the book out of your head and onto paper. For so many of us the fear of the blank page has us procrastinating forever. Writing a book is like eating an elephant. If you try to do it all at once, it's too much, too big and you don't even know where to start. So what we need to do is take little tiny bites of the elephant, one at a time.

When I work with my private coaching clients, the first thing that we do is a "brain dump." This means that you just write down everything that you can think of. At this point we're not worried about validity or censoring. No decisions need to be made, if you think it, write it down. Don't even try to write full sentences, just

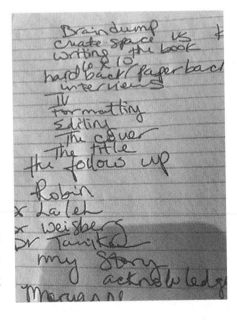

throw down words or phrases. The best advice I can give you for this step is don't overthink, don't analyze, don't prioritize, just get everything out of your head and onto the paper. I promise there will be plenty of time for organizing later.

Once you've done your brain dump, now is the time to judge, organize, and classify. You may see that some things are actually the same topic in different words and some are really totally unrelated, or so big that they warrant their own book. I know, right now it's really hard to imagine wanting to write a second book, but most of my clients end up becoming serial authors. Like childbirth, you forget the pain. If you're a guy, that analogy may not make sense to you, but ask any mom you know :-).

Back to the brain dump, once you've judged, classified, organized it, then you want to use that as your loose outline.

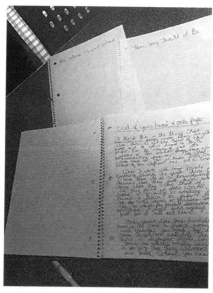

At this point, what I do is take a notebook, (remember, I'm old school that way), and write each phrase across the top of the page. If I think it's going to be a longer topic, I might skip a couple of pages before writing the next one.

Then I do one topic per writing session. I may do a few writing sessions a day, but for each one, I make my goal just one topic. I'm still not really editing or censoring myself, I'm just trying to explore each topic.

Some of my clients find that it's easier to process verbally. For you are such a client, I would have you dictate each topic, one at a time. You can use your phone's native voice memo feature, or use an app like Otter or Dragonspeak. This can be done while you're in the car, the bathroom, waiting for something, taking a walk, or whatever. Since you're only doing one topic at a time, it's in small bite size chunks, 5 minutes here, 7 minutes there.

If you're using an app that records and transcribes, great! Check for errors first, and then read through for clarity and missing info.

Remember that the way we speak and the way we write are different, so make sure you take the time to translate it into a written discourse.

If you're using an app that doesn't transcribe for you, there's a great service called Rev.com where you can upload your file and get the transcript back the next day. Some of my clients need an interviewer to bring out their ideas, so I interview them, record the interviews and then send those interviews out for transcription.

Another method for getting the content out of your head is to make a list of the questions that you hear the most from your clients. I bet if you took 10 seconds right now, you could think of a whole bunch of them. Then, make another list of the questions that you WISH your clients would ask you.

For example, in my first book, *The Ultimate Guide To Inflating Your Tradeshow Profits,* one of the most frequently asked questions is "How long do balloons last?" One of the questions that I wish they would ask is "What are best practices for balloons outdoors?" Both of those questions were answered in the book.

This method is especially good for doctors and other experts who constantly have to train their clients/ patients. For example, if you are a functional medicine doctor, how many times have you heard the question "What even is functional medicine?"

Once you decide what questions you wish they would ask, follow the same steps above to write or dictate the answers a little at a time.

Another way to get the information out is to interview other people. These could be other leaders in your field, or, as I do later in this book, it could be your clients. Prepare a list of questions and conduct your interviews utilizing a recordable medium. Go To Meeting, Zoom, and Webinar Jam are all software that work well for this application. Then get it all transcribed and edit it for clarity and missing information.

After you have all the transcriptions, you need to collate them and figure out how each section relates to the others. At this point, you may need to devise some transitions between sections to connect them or fill in the holes.

The next step is to send it to editing. If at all possible, get someone who matches your target customer to read it, so that you can make sure that it makes sense to someone who is not familiar with the topic and may not understand the jargon. Unless you are writing for an "in" audience, you want to make it easy for lay people to understand it.

After all this, you will want to send it to a professional editor or proofreader who can catch the errors that no one else saw. We'll talk more about editing in another section.

EDITING

Editing is really important. You should read through the text a few times before passing it off to an editor. You really want to get some extra eyeballs on your book because after looking at it over and over, your brain stats to see what it wants to see and not what's actually there. That's how it can happen that once the book is printed, a typo that was never there before suddenly jumps off the page.

I always recommend to my clients that you give the first round of editing to friends who are representative of your target market. That way they'll be able to catch gaps in information or unclear jargon. After you have their input, give the book draft to an editor who will read for clarity and cohesiveness. Finally, you want a proofreader who will check for grammar, syntax, spelling, and typos.

There are different levels of editing, the highest being a research and copy editor. This editor is going to fact check for you and rewrite sections, move things around, and basically redo your book for you.

The simplest form of editing is proofreading.

I offer various editing packages for my clients. For proof reading/ light editing, it's included in many of the packages, whereas the higher level of editing is priced according to the number of pages and writing style. In such a case, we need to see the manuscript before quoting the job.

I thought that it would be valuable to hear from an editor on what you can do to make it easier for your editor to do a good job for you, so I reached out to one of the very best editors I know, 50+ year journalist, editor and my dad, Don Harrison. Here are the tips he shared with me:

"Read aloud what you write. If it's easy to say, it's easy to read."

"Write in active voice"

"Try to minimize subordinate clauses and run-on sentences, i.e. *The dog, who was running down the street, peed on my ficus, which I had planted three years ago.*" Yeah, I'm guilty of doing that one a lot, lol.

"Use parallelism with verbs, i.e. *He ran down the street, jumped on the trampoline, and ate his custard pie.* 'Ran,' 'jumped' and 'ate' are all the same tense."

"The other mistake that people make is mixing subject and verb tenses, ie *They eats cherry pie,* which should be *They eat cherry pie.*"

"Be consistent on using or not using the Oxford comma, (which is the comma before the last item in a series.)" At Oxford, a sentence might read: "I love dogs, cats, and little canaries." Elsewhere, the same sentence would read: "I love dogs, cats and little canaries."

And lastly, "Refer to people in second references as "who" and not "that", for example, *The fireman who [not that] rescued me was strong.*"

FORMATTING

If you're really a DIY-er, then maybe you want to tackle the formatting yourself, but honestly, if you value your time and sanity this is a good place to spend some money..

However, just in case you're a masochist of sorts, here are some guidelines for you:

Kindle is best in a word doc. Here's the important thing about Kindle, it's like a long form HTML page from the 90s, simple is better.

Every device will display things differently; the iPhone shows it differently than a tablet which is different from a computer, which is different from an actual Kindle device. Also the reader can change the font size. All this to say, don't worry about pagination, it's mostly out of your control. In the places that you need it to start on a new "page," like at the beginning of a chapter, you need to insert a hard page break.

Each chapter title should be set as an H1 (Heading 1) tag. This will allow you to create a clickable table of contents, which is really important for Kindle.

Since Kindle doesn't have pages in the traditional sense, there are also no headers or footers.

Photos in Kindle should be either Jpeg or Png, inserted between paragraphs and centered. Don't use text wrap, it will not show up well.

Avoid tables and call-out boxes if at all possible.

The table of contents should be "custom" and then remove the page numbers. You can upload the word doc to KDP. Launch the previewer in KDP to check it for obvious issues or hidden formatting.

The final document should be uploaded as a word doc. Once upon a time it had to be converted to a .Mobi file, but kdp has really improved its ability to take a word doc and convert it. Do not upload a PDF. It will not work well and the table of contents won't be clickable.

PAPERBACK FORMATTING

This is a different animal all together. It's best done in a graphics program like In Design, and the outputted file should be a high resolution PDF. The main thing to remember here is that the margins and gutters need to be different on the right side and the left side to account for the spine.

The most common book size, or "trim size" is 6 x 9. Often the odd number pages will have the name of the book in the header, and the even number pages will have the name of the chapter.

Page numbers should be on the bottom outer corner of each page, or in the center.

We use In-design, a graphics program, to lay out the pages. I think there is more control, and it turns out a better product to use a graphics program than to do it in word.

Rather than go into all the (many) specifics of how to format, here is a link to a page on the CreateSpace website that will give you those details: https://www.createspace.com/Special/Enterprise/Publisher/submission_guidelines.jsp

THE LAUNCH

often get asked about whether it's better to do a pre-release or a full launch.

Once upon a time pre-release was only available to the biggest publishers. It was only a couple of years ago that Amazon opened up pre-release to self-published authors who utilize Kindle.

The cool thing about doing a pre-release is that you can make your book a bestseller before you've even finished writing it. Another advantage is that if you are a person who does well under pressure and with a hard deadline, this will spur you to action. I do all of my books as a pre-release because I'm one of those people who needs the pressure of a hard deadline to get it done.

If, on the other hand, you're a person who gets stressed out by hard deadlines, then I would say that you should take your time and finish your book, and then release it.

I will tell you this though, 100% of my clients who do a pre-release finish their book and make it a reality. On the other hand, only 35% of the people I've spoken to who prefer to wait to do a full release actually end up writing their book. Life happens, and if you don't make your book a priority, it will forever remain just a dream.

So, if you would feel more comfortable doing a full release; that is, waiting until the book is completed to launch it, then make sure that you set deadlines for yourself and work with someone for accountability. That way the book will stay a priority, even when life gets messy.

Shameless plug, that's what I help my private coaching clients with. I keep you on track and accountable with individualized weekly goals.

AFTER THE BOOK

Let's talk about the hard part- marketing the book. Unfortunately "If you build it, they will come" is rarely true. You must also market it, heavily.

First, figure out what is your goal for this book? Do you have a message you're trying to get out and magnify? Or are you planning to give the book away as a part of your marketing shock and awe package?

Either way, your book can open doors for you.

Before your book is released start building the buzz with your tribe. Tell them that you're writing a book, ask them what they want to know, send them updates about how it's going, and post photos of you in action. Get them excited and ready to buy on launch day.

Once the book is out, send out press releases announcing it. You can do this through PRWeb.com, ReleaseWire, and PR Newswire by Cision.

Then, start trying to book yourself on radio and TV to talk about your book. This is best done by direct email or phone calls to the shows' producers. Let them know that you are the author of a new book, (or better yet, a new bestselling book,) and that you have some valuable tips to share with their audience. Do your homework and know what the show format is and how you fit into it before you pitch them. A finance show is not going to be interested in a book on cat care for example.

Get media training if you can. This will ensure that once you get booked, you'll be a good guest who may be invited back.

Reach out to your local bookstores and see if you can put your book in their store on consignment and if you can set up a book signing.

Put copies of your book in your office and offer them to all of your patients/ clients.

Make some videos showing the book and post on You-Tube and Facebook.

A great video to make is your unboxing video- that is when you get your book for the first time, and you make a video of you opening the package and seeing it for the first time. It's a really emotional and joyous moment and goes a long way to humanize you and to get others interested in your excitement.

If you want to use the book to get speaking engagements, send a copy of your book to the person in charge of the event or conference at which you want to speak. It's a huge credibility booster. And if you're worried about getting past the gatekeeper, send it as a gift directly from Amazon.

A popular way to get attention to your book is to do a "Free + Shipping" campaign. Basically you offer your book to people (through social media and email marketing) as free + shipping. Most of the time authors charge from $7- $10 for the "free + shipping" price. This won't make you money, but will cover the cost of the book and shipping so that you can get it into the hands of more readers and prospects, thereby magnifying your message.

THE AUTHORS

I could go on and on about the benefits of publishing a book, but instead of giving you my opinion, I interviewed some of my clients. Here you can see, in their own words, what they got out of writing a book, and how they did it.

My clients always amaze me with their awesomeness, and the nine in this book are no exception. They run the gamut from doctors, to business people, to etiquette experts, to domestic violence survivor advocates. And then there's me, the balloon lady. If you think that you have nothing to say, or that your business is different, I'm here to tell you, it's not. You are an expert on your industry, and it's time to let the world know. Every business can benefit from writing a book! So enjoy these stories of some of my very favorite authors!

Book III.

DR. LALEH SHABAN
– *The Fountain of Youth*
& Eternal Health

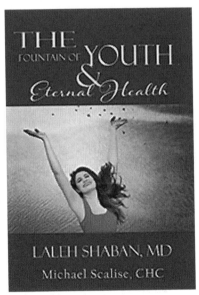

Dr. Laleh Shaban is an incredible doctor, woman, and success story. She's triple board certified, in internal medicine, geriatrics, and metabolic medicine, and moved from being an MD to being a functional medicine doctor. She's also certified in Metabolic Cardiology, Bio-Identical Hormone Replacement Therapy, Bone Marrow Stem Cell, O-shot, P-shot & Cosmetic Procedures. She's a force to be reckoned with and is someone who inspires me to no end. If she were geographically only a little closer to me, she would be my doctor as well. I just don't have the words to express how impressed I have been with Dr. Shaban in the time that I've known her.

Sandi: The first thing that I want to talk to you about is your writing process. That is how you actually went from the idea of the book to the written word and to having the manuscript. What was your process?

Laleh: Okay. I had been invited to speak at Harvard, and before I left [Clint] notified me that I have to have a book, and I had never had a book. I had to come with a quick idea and a quick publication of the book. I started talking about my practice and my patients. The book is really stories of patients. Because it's stories of patients, it has had such an amazing impact, because apparently people love reading stories. They don't want to just read a book. They want to read stories, because it helps them remember the message. Since I've written the book, it has been so powerful. I've had people come and say, "You are the change of medicine." I'm a revolutionary type of person, in that I feel that I'm going to make a difference, and the world is going to change.

The feedback I'm getting is not anything like I expected. I expected just a book for Harvard, so that I could comply with requirements that I'm supposed to comply with. It's been an amazing experience.

Sandi: You did your book as a pre-release, right? Which means that you put it up on Amazon, and people started purchasing it, and then you had a very strict deadline in terms of when it had to be done. Did you just sit down at the computer and start writing the stories? Did you dictate it? How did you actually get it down on paper?

Laleh: I was coming back from CNN, and I had like a seven-hour flight. I started just writing, and I didn't stop. I wrote most of my book on the flight back. Then, of course, when I brought it back and had my staff type it, it was a lot shorter than I needed to have it. I guess we wanted 100 pages, and all those scribbles I had done came up to like 30 pages.

I involved my husband, who also is a certified health coach in my practice. He see patients, and he has a lot of experience and knowledge. We basically decided to expand on parts of the book, expand on portions of what we thought would be really helpful for people to know. We started talking not about just the stories, but adding some statistics and some facts that would really stand out in people's minds. That's what we did. So, we made the deadline. It's just been amazing. The feedback, as I said, has been just something I didn't expect.

Sandi: Before writing the book, where were you? I don't mean physically where were you, but I mean like with your business, with your life. What was going on around you?

Laleh: When I give somebody a high blood pressure medication, I'm really not curing them. I'm just putting a Band-Aid on their problem, because if they don't take their medication, the next day their blood pressure is going to come up, so I didn't heal that person. They weren't born with high blood pressure. Something happened as they were living their life that got them to where they are with all these conditions, so why not go back and figure out what happened, address it at that level, and try to heal the condition at a cellular level, rather than at a medication level or a 'Band-Aid?' With that, I started getting my board certification in metabolic medicine and nutrition, which is functional medicine. I started converting my practice to a functional medicine practice, which has been extremely successful.

Meanwhile, about in 2005, I had 4,000 medical patients. That's when I was in mainstream medicine, and I was taking insurance. I was working

40

20 hours a day. I was starting at 4:00 in the morning in the intensive care unit at the hospital, seeing my comatose patients. The time was conve-
nient for them as one doesn't wake them up. Then
I started at my office at 8:00, and I worked till
midnight, and then started again at 4:00 in the
morning. I did that for eight years, but it was
draining. I told my husband, "I just don't know if
I can do this anymore. I'm not seeing the kids. I'm
missing out on them growing up." My husband
would bring them to the hospital for me to hug
them and tell them I loved them. I decided something has to change.

My husband said, "How about concierge medical
practice?" At that time, I studied about concierge
medical practice. Instead of having 4,000 patients
covered under an insurance program, which
could be slow and uncertain, I decided to take
care of only 200 patients, who would pay pay up-
front.

I sent letters to 400 patients saying that I'm sorry
I'm not going to be able to take care of you guys. I
had resources that I sent them to. Then I sent another letter two weeks later to 600 patients saying,
I am going to start a new practice. This is how
I'm going to do it. Here are my conditions, and if
you want to be a patient, first come, first served,
and this is my fee.

Not only did I fill my practice within three weeks, but I had for years a waiting list of over 500 people who would come and say, "Has anybody died? Can I enter your practice? Has anybody left?" Luckily, people were living a good long life, and I wasn't really losing any patients. Once in a while, if a patient of mine wanted their husband or daughter to join the practice I would take them in.

I was triple board certified in internal medicine, geriatrics, and then metabolic medicine or functional medicine. When I decided to switch, I started taking all my patients off medication. Some of them were on 20, 21 medications. Eventually, after a year, I would get them to one or zero, and they felt the best they've ever felt. Then I would bring all these other things to my practice to support them, because you can't just take people off medication. It's not safe to do it that way.

Some patients had leaky gut syndrome. They weren't absorbing their nutrients. If you don't absorb your nutrients, your body gains weight. I had a lot of people suffering from obesity, because they were so nutritionally deficient. Your body understands you're not getting nutrients and because your gut doesn't work, your brain keeps telling your stomach, "Eat more. Eat more." Instead of getting nutrients, you gain weight, and you gain fat.

Then I started my weight loss program, because my husband was on 10 different medications. He was over 300 pounds. He was so fatigued and tired. I would come home, and he could barely move. I remember one day I looked at him, and I thought, "This is the love of my life, and I'm hoping one day he can walk our daughter down the aisle, but it doesn't look like he's going to make it." At that time is I thought, "Mainstream medicine has failed him. I need to do something different. I need to get him off medication." That's when the urge of functional medicine came into my life. I decided I'm going to do everything in my power to help him.

I started working with him. I came up with a weight loss program. It's called Shaban's Method. With the weight loss program, it was so successful, he lost 70 pounds, and he got off all his medications. It was so amazingly successful that I decided, if I can help him, I'm sure I can help everybody else. Then I started applying it to my patients. They did great. Then I went kind of viral with it. Our weight loss program is one of the things that I do in my practice. I have a very successful weight loss program. It's a six-month program. My health coaches run it. We do special things. There are different phases.

While we're healing people's guts, we're putting them on intravenous (IV) nutrients, so we have an IV center. To get people off medications, such as Vicodin, or other pain medications that make people groggy, or have accidents, or become constipated, or feel horrible, I started bringing things to help with pain management. I brought ozone therapy and various cutting edge technologies that we are utilize in my practice. I'm also address people's hormones, because every sign of aging is a hormone deficiency. I have a bioidentical hormone practice. Of course, I have a cosmetic practice. My cosmetic practice is the most thriving practice in my town, in my county. We have lasers and a bunch of things that others do not yet have.

It takes years for others to catch up with us, because I believe in bringing in the cutting edge technology to the practice. We're among the first practices to introduce anything, such as PRP, which is platelet rich plasma, also known as vampire facials. We did that like five, six years ago. Now it's becoming really well known, and now people are getting it done everywhere.

I have five or six different wings to my practice. When I wrote this book, I decided I was going to give it as a gift to all 200 medical patients who are in my concierge practice.. I had a book signing. I invited them. I gave them a book. I signed it for them. I asked them for feedback. I said, "I really need feedback. This is the first book I've written, so I can always get better. Please let me know what

I can do to be better. Don't be shy to let me know that it was a horrible book, because there's always room for improvement." To my surprise, because I really wrote the book so fast, we really spent just four months on that book. To my surprise, I have been having people calling me, buying 15, sending it to their friends or buying it and bringing it for me to sign for their family members or friends.

It's become a big thing, to a point that I had the local TV people and radio contact me, and they wanted me to talk about my mission and why I wrote the book and what do I see as the impact of the book on people. The first chapter says don't trust your doctor. Of course, I'm a physician, and I'm a physician that's triple boarded. I'm a physician who does so many different things. If I'm saying don't trust your doctor, something is not right. I love my patients, and my patients love me. We have a really good relationship. For me to tell people, don't trust your doctor, it's because I've seen so many mistakes, so many mistakes that nobody knows, because they cover it. CDC does not report #3 cause of death in the United States is medical mistake. #1 is heart attacks and heart disease. #2 is cancer, and #3 is medical mistakes, whether it's the doctor who made a mistake or pharmacist or it was the wrong drug that the patient took or it was a side effect of the medication, that patient died. Numerous different things, but it's medical mistakes.

I think people should take charge, because with doctors who practice under insurance constraints they have to see like 30 - 40 patients a day. That means they have five minutes with each patient. That means that they don't even have time to listen to the patient. On the other hand, patients go in expecting. They've paid a $15 co-pay, they better get something out of it. The doctor says, "You have a headache. Here is a prescription for Imitrex." The patient takes the Imitrex. Then they get constipated. Come back, "You have constipation. This is a medication for constipation." Then they come back, because they have another side effect from the constipation medication. Before you know it, you're on 21 different drugs, simply because your doctor never took the time to talk to you to find out what's going on.

Also, I have patients who, for example, go to surgery, and it's unnecessary surgery. They don't know they have other choices. For example, I draw people's blood, spin it, and get the growth factors, called PRP, and inject it into their joints. That reverses the damage. It regrows the tissues. If you don't have to have shoulder surgery for rotator cuff tear, or knee replacement, it's like an hour procedure in my practice. No pain. Nothing. You walk out of there. Whereas with surgery, you're at risk. Every time you go under anesthesia there is risk of dementia 10 years later, all these toxicity in your brain that can cause Parkinson's 10 years later. There is risk of pulmonary embolism, which is blood clot, in your lungs or in your legs, DVT. There is a risk of, of course, eight weeks loss of work, because you just had knee surgery. Then there are all the expenses and dangers of physical therapy.

People don't know you can just do the same thing in an hour in an office and there you go. Nobody gives you those choices. Doctors either don't know -- they don't know what they don't know -- or if they know, they are not practicing it themselves, because they don't have time to go the certification because they have to see 40 patients a day. They don't have time to even read. So, they're not going to promote it. They're going to try to talk their patients out of it.

I've seen that. I've seen people who go to the orthopedic surgeon and say, "Dr. Shaban does PRP and joint injections. What do you think?" They say, "No. Don't do it. It's not a good thing." Either they don't know about the procedure, or they don't want to lose a patient. What they are not thinking is about the patient. They're thinking about their own pocket. That's some doctors, not all the doctors. I have a lot of respect for physicians.

This country is the best country when it comes to acute diseases. That means if you dropped right down with a heart attack, I'm not going to sit there and talk about your gut and your diet and how we can change that. Of course, we're going to do everything to bring you back. This country is amazing for that. It's one of the best. If you're going to have any acute condition, this is the place you want to be. Within seconds you're in the ER. 911 is called. The ambulance is there. The paramedics already have a line in you and oxygen. Your EKG is done, and on the way to the hospital you're already getting orders from the ER physician, and you're stabilized or close to being stabilized by the time you get to the ER.

Sandi: Talking about the impact of your book, both on you and your clients and the world, you were hugely successful before writing the book. Really, you were magnifying your message and increasing your impact out in the world with your book.

Laleh: Yes. I didn't realize I was doing that. I just thought, honestly, I was just writing a book that I had to write to be able to speak at Harvard, because that was their requirement that I was told I had to have. Even though I wrote it really fast, in four months, and didn't put a whole lot of thought into it, I had stories of my patients that I could share with the world. The stories, I think the stories are so strong and so empowering to so many people, because they identify. If I just give statistics, nobody is going to remember.

I'm giving a lot of talks locally, and people come back to tell me the impact of the stories they heard. "When you talked about that patient of yours who did this, I went home and told my family you should be checked for this and this and this." Those are the stories that are empowering them to want to take their health in their own hands, because they saw what a patient went through.

Sandi: Do you have any stories of a specific impact or incident that happened because of your book?

Laleh: The book had been out only been three or four months when I had a lady who came to me and said, "Oh my God, Dr. Shaban, I called my mother-in-law, who's 90 years old. She's very independent, but she's had rotator cuff tears and nobody will do surgery on this woman. She can't sleep. She can't roll on that side. She cannot lift her arm. Besides the arm, she is a very active woman, but it's affecting her life so bad. If she takes medication, she's groggy and she's at risk of falls, so she tries not to take medication, but then she's in so much pain." She said, "I read your book, and I found out about PRP and stem cells in the shoulder. I told my mother-in-law, and she is looking into it to see who are the doctors near her that do this, so that she can get that done." She said, "I'm so grateful for knowing this option existed. I didn't know."

We've had people who didn't know about O-Shot or P-Shot, which is the same thing for men. They have also come and said, "Because of the book, I've learned all these existed. I didn't know. I thought I had to have surgery and a lift and mesh and all that for my urinary problems."

So, yes, it has. I have patients who come in and say, "My husband asked his doctor about a 24-hour blood pressure monitor, but the doctor didn't know anything about it." Our weight loss program has picked up even more, we're even busier, because of people who have read it and passed it onto a friend. Things like that, yes, it has had impact.

It had only been on the market for four months now, but it started a big buzz, because the first chapter says do not trust your doctor. That is like, what?

Sandi: That's a great opening line. Talking again about the writing and publishing process, what was the hardest part of it for you?

Laleh: I think you guys made it super easy. I honestly had never published a book before, because I thought it was going to be so painful, so time con-suming, and so involved, involving my time. I do so much. I honestly do not have a whole lot of time to dedicate to one more thing. With that said, I had not even thought about doing a book.

When I wrote it, and it went so smooth with you guys, everybody is asking me for my second book. I have so many people calling and saying, "When are you writing? I can't wait for your next book to come out."

My husband and I are talking about coming up with the next book, but we haven't decided if it's going to be the continuation of the first book. We didn't include a lot of things, because we didn't have time to really think about a lot of the stories that I'd remember in the last 22 years of my practice. We could do a Volume 2 or Part 2 or continuation. My husband does want to talk about heart disease, because that's the #1 killer in this country. Again, there's so many options nobody knows. We can reverse heart disease.

With that said, you guys made it so easy for us that now I see light at the end of the tunnel. Now I see that when I'm ready to write the second book I can always pick up the phone, call Sandi, and things are done so smoothly. It was a wonderful experience.

Sandi: What advice do you have for other experts, or even other doctors, who are thinking about publishing a book, or aren't sure if they want to?

Laleh: I would tell anybody, don't be overwhelmed. If you have a good team, just start writing, and then leave it up to the team of knowledgeable experts

Sandi: Thank you. Is there anything else that you'd like to share, or that I should have asked, but I didn't?

Laleh: I have to tell you that you guys were really prompt. I wasn't, but you guys were. You were on case, which made it really good for us not to procrastinate. As I said, I do like 200 different things a day. If I don't get reminders that there's a deadline, you need to make it, then I'll push that back. I won't get to it till later. Just getting that feedback from you guys saying there's a deadline you really need to get this to me by this and this time would bring that as a more priority on top of everything else. Then, if I would delay things I would get another call. I thought that was extremely helpful. It was a very positive thing, that experience that I had, that made me actually get the book published rather than trying to procrastinate with it.

Sandi: My last question is what website would you like me to promote in the book? Where do you want me to send people to learn more about you and your practice?

Laleh: It's www.ReviveMdMedicalGroup.com. Revive MD Medical Group is the name of my practice.

DR. VERNE WEISBERG
- *Face Your Future*

Dr. Verne Weisberg is among other things a Yale-trained cosmetic surgeon. He began his practice as an assistant professor at Yale, but found his true calling in serving the patients who put their trust in him. His biggest joy is in seeing the transformation of his patients as they recover their sense of self and their self-confidence.

Sandi: I want to talk a little bit about your writing process, that is how you went from the idea and the blank page to the actual written word.

Verne: Great question. First, I sat down, and I thought about what it was that I could contribute, and I thought about all the questions I get. A lot are the same questions, after 30 years of doing this thing. I thought, how about a guide for somebody who's considering getting cosmetic surgery, because you're out there, and you don't know what's available. How do I go about it? Where do I go? What's right for me? What questions should I ask? I thought, let's think about the questions, and what do I tell everybody so that they have very few questions after we sit down and talk.

I sat down, and I made basically a table of contents of the sorts of things that would be necessary to cover. Then, I dictated into my iPhone each chapter, basically as if I were talking to someone. As each chapter was dictated, when I got through it, I uploaded it to a transcriptionist, and then when the transcription came back I went through and edited it as best I could. I asked a friend to discuss an area in which he was an expert. After finishing the chapters, I put the book together with the table of contents. Then, I had someone edit it. So, that's how I wrote it.

Sandi: About how long would you say, start to finish, the process took you?

Verne: It took me a long time to get started, which is true of most people unless they have a burning desire to write a book, which most people do not. Sometimes people say "write a book, so you become an expert." Obviously, you should be an expert before you write the book. The book just gives you additional credibility. I needed something that gave me a timeline, and I had a three-month window to write the book. It was a short book.

Sandi: We did the pre-release on it, right?

Verne: We did. Yes.

Sandi: So, that's what gave you your timeline and your hard deadline there, right?

Verne: Exactly. I almost forgot about that. I knew there was some reason that I had to finish it.

Sandi: That's right. Those darn Amazon deadlines.

Verne: Right. It worked out very well. Fortunately, I had an expert helping as to how to get the process done, because I probably wouldn't have figured it out myself. Maybe I would have, but it seemed overwhelming to me.

Sandi: I bet you could have figured it out, but I'm glad that I was able to shorten the learning curve for you.

Verne: There's so many things that we can do, but why would we try to if we're not necessarily an expert at it? Right?

Sandi: Right.

Verne: I can probably make a soufflé, but I'm sure that if I really needed to have a good soufflé I'd get somebody who knew what they were doing.

Sandi: Why did you write your book?

Verne: I wrote the book to use as a guideline, and also as marketing material. Initially to give out to people who were considering working with me, so that they would have a better idea of who I was before they came to see me. So that by reading the book, they were not going in and going, who are you, and why should I listen to you? After they've read your book, or at least they know you've written a book, whether they've read it or not, they don't ask that question. That also helps to prequalify the people you talk to, because you only have so much time in a day, or your life. You don't want to talk to people who aren't really interested that much in talking to you, or don't feel like you are going to give them the information or the service that they want.

That was basically why I wrote the book. I heard that I should write the book, and then our mutual friend insisted that I write the book and helped me come up with the title.

Sandi: What has been the effect of having a book, on your business, in your life, on your relationship with patients? Just in any way that you can quantify the effect of it.

Verne: The effect is certainly people are excited to meet me. They're very impressed that I wrote a book. The surprise effect was that people actually read it. In fact, I had one person who read it twice. Maybe more than one, but one who I know of who told me that she read it twice. That was great, but I didn't formally track the overall effect. I sent this person a book. How many people did I send the book? How many people felt like the book helped? It's just one of those things that you put in your "shock and awe package" that helps. It just makes things better. It helps you to stand out, because not everybody writes a book.

They might have the idea to write a book, but, as I said, it's not easy to sit down and figure out ways to get leverage on yourself to get it down. The more people that you involve in that, the more likely you are to actually do it. Just doing it by yourself, it's hard to get enough leverage to get up every day and say, I'm going to spend this amount of time doing it, and whatever progress I make is progress. That's separate.

Sandi: Have you found that it saves time on the initial consultation with clients if you give them a book, or if they're read the book, and they're better informed from the get-go?

Verne: I thought that might be it, but I haven't noticed. I can't tell you that that's true. It seems like that would happen, but it mostly makes it easier for someone to establish the relationship, and people are more likely to listen to what you have to say. They figure that you know what you're talking about, because you wrote a book.

Sandi: You literally wrote the book on the topic. Yes.

Verne: It doesn't hurt that through the prelaunch I wound up being a national and international bestseller. That's something that nobody ever can take away from you. I'm a bestselling author. I have a friend who's a very serious author or novels that are amazing, and we talked about this. I said, you know, I am an author. I did write a book that was self-published, and it was a bestseller. He goes, you're an author. You're a bestselling author. That's pretty good. I like that. It was good information.

It is real. You don't need to have an asterisk next to your name that I was a bestselling author, but we figured out some way to do that. I'm not on the *New York Times* bestseller list, like my friend is, but that's fine.

I think it's made that difference in that it helps me to stand out, because nobody else has written a book. Certainly no one in my region. That's more likely to be read than an article in a trade journal or professional journal by somebody who's going to be your customer. You write articles in professional or trade journals for whatever reason, but what happens is you're impressing your peers, which is very nice, but they're not going to buy anything from you. They're not feeding you. From my standpoint, writing a book was very helpful for marketing. In fact, I've run out of them. I have to print them up again to give to people.

Sandi: You mentioned putting your book in your shock and awe box and using it for marketing. How else are you using your book? Has it helped you book speaking engagements or tv appearances?

Verne: It was going to, and then the areas that were interested then found that they weren't interested, or at the time didn't need something, or they were more interested in having somebody local talk about what I was going to talk about. I did get invitations to book talks. It was tough for me following up. I did follow up, to be able also to go out West was tough. I had invitations to go to New Mexico and Oregon and California. I live in Maine. The only one close was Connecticut, and they were like, when you have the book launch, if you happen to do be something in our area, we'd love to have you come in. I didn't go down there to do that. That was me, but I could have. I did have invitations to talk about the book.

Sandi: You haven't tried to get on your local tv in Maine?

Verne: I have done that. Absolutely. Many times.

Sandi: You've had a relationship with those producers even before your book then.

Verne: Yes.

Sandi: Nice. Do they promote your book when you go on there now?

Verne: They do.

Sandi: Awesome. What was the hardest part or the biggest challenge of the writing and publishing process for you?

Verne: Sitting down and doing it.

Sandi: Just getting started and getting it done.

Verne: Yes. Like anything. I find that with every aspect of anything that I write, and I do a lot of writing for myself, to think things through. When you start to sit down, what comes out first isn't necessarily great, or even palatable, but as you do it, you start to get some flow. It's sort of like if you're going to go for a run. You wouldn't just jump out the door and be right up to speed. You warm up a little bit. Some days it's easier than others to do so. That's the same with writing, from my experience.

That sounded good. Didn't it?

Sandi: It did. I mean, if you had to do it all over again, would you do it again?

Verne: Yes. In fact, I'm thinking about what my next book is going to be.

Sandi: What advice do you have for other experts who want to publish a book, or who have been thinking about it?

Verne: Do it. Don't think. The advice that we all think it has to be perfect, and it doesn't.

Sandi: That's great advice.

Verne: A plan well-executed is better than a well-considered plan that isn't executed. You really have to do something, and if you wait for it to be perfect it never will be, and it'll never get done. If you really feel badly about it, you can say, there may be some mistakes here. Sometimes my mind goes faster than my words or my writing, but I apologize if there's a few errors here or there. I'm doing my best to give you what I think is important. It doesn't have to be perfect, just get it done.

Think about what you would want. Be your client. Be the person who's going to read it and really empathize and think about what you would want to know, or what you would think would be interesting, or what you would think would be valuable or useful. Keith Cunningham says the secret to success is find out what they want, go out and get it, and give it to them. That's it. That's the secret to successful business. Find out what they want, go out and get it, and give it to them. That's the secret to a successful relationship as well. Just saying.

Sandi: Is there anything else you'd like to share that I should have asked about that I didn't?

Verne: How do you feel when the book shows up on your doorstep?

Sandi: How did you feel?

Verne: It's pretty amazing. It's like nothing else before. You go, wait a minute, is that real? Is that really me? How did that happen? It's pretty spectacular how you feel when it finally shows up. You go through a lot of stuff figuring out the cover, figuring out the colors, figuring out the print, which has nothing to do with writing it. There's all the other stuff. When it all comes together, it's a pretty big project, and you have to celebrate. I guess, what I would tell people is don't forget to celebrate. Celebrate when you finish a sentence. Celebrate. It doesn't have to be a huge celebration, but have some way to celebrate when you're done, because we never celebrate enough.

Sandi: That's another really good point. I think all too often we keep our focus on what we think we should have done, and not what we accomplished.

Verne: Exactly.

Sandi: That's a great point. My very last question is what is the website that you'd like me to promote in the book?

Verne: I sold my business.

Sandi: Congratulations.

Verne: I'm still working though at www.MainePlasticSurgery.com .

Sandi: Great. I'll put that as a place that people can find out more, or redirect them to the sales page for the book itself on Amazon, whichever you prefer.

Verne: Either way works, or both. I would do www. VerneWeisberg.com

DR. CATRISE AUSTIN
– *Get Smiled!*

D r. Catrise Austin is truly the celebrity dentist. Her patient roster reads like the who's who of hip hop. She was immortalized in the song *Bodak Yellow* by Cardi B. If you don't know who that is, that's ok, ask your kids or grandkids :-). Beyond being just a dentist, she's also an entrepreneur who has recently brought out her own line of dental products like activated charcoal teeth whitener and some other home teeth whitening products as well. At the time of this writing she has 2 best selling books, and is already working on the third.

Sandi: Let's talk about both your books. I want to know about your writing process and how you went from the idea to the written word.

Catrise: The first book called *Get Smiled*, I really wrote it college style. I came up with an outline, and wrote chapter by chapter. Well, I take that back. This will be really my third book. The first one was called *Five Steps to a Hollywood A-List Smile*, that I think I released around 2011. That one was straight college, stay up all night writing a term paper, and basically putting it into a book form. I had a publisher for that book, one of those intermediate publishers where you pay them a lot of money, and they kind of guide you through the process, and you have an "official publisher."

The second book, *Get Smiled*, which you helped me go to #1 with, I took a totally different approach. After learning more about marketing, I took the frequently asked questions that I get every day about cosmetic dentistry, and made those chapters by subject. That way, it was more relevant to consumers. They could just go to the question that's been on their mind, and you have it.

Being that I talk about this stuff every day in my office, it was a lot easier to do it in that format. Because if you think about, particularly if you're a service provider, it was just really an extended version of a brochure or business card, just answering their questions.

The first book, I was thinking about being a published author. The second book, I was thinking about it as a marketing tool. Having been an author before, I realized that in today's world you really don't make a lot of money on books. It's more a marketing tool. Keeping that in mind, I really approached the second, and this third book on charcoal teeth whitening, as a more consumer, answering your questions, extended brochure kind of tool.

Sandi: In the last two, both of them, you sat down and figured out, what questions do I keep hearing? How can I help give clarity on this topic?

Catrise: Exactly.

Sandi: Nice. You answered this, but I just want to go a little bit more on why you wrote your book, or what you were hoping to get out of it. I don't know if it was the same for all three, or if you have different goals for each one.

Catrise: I would say, for me, I wrote all my books keeping the consumer in mind and wanting to disseminate information and answer questions that they may not have the answers to, because dentistry, unfortunately, still isn't that topic that you get on news stories and in magazines. People do have myths in their head about dentistry, and they don't know where to turn to for some of the questions, particularly cosmetic dentistry.

I wrote it really for the consumers to have the answers that they needed in the most layman terms that I could put it. There are some doctors who talk about bicuspids and all kinds of technical terms, and you still don't have the answers that you're looking for. That's my goal. To really break it down. Even a two or three year old could understand it. Hopefully, I accomplished that.

Sandi: Where were you before writing your book? I don't mean physically, like I was in my living room, but I mean like in your business, in your life. Basically, I want to see the transformation trajectory of the effects of your book.

Catrise: Business-wise, I had already established, I started my business. This is actually my 20th year anniversary, so I started my business in 1998. From the start, I had gotten a lot of PR. By the time I wrote the first book in 2011, it was kind of the missing link. Some other big cosmetic dentists who have gained some notoriety, like Dr. Bill Dorfman on *Extreme Makeover* wrote a book on the billion-dollar smile. Some of my other really big competitors had books and products, hence me really this year coming out with my product.

It seemed to be a part of the formula that you're an author if you're an expert in your field. I felt like that was the one thing that I was missing.

One part of it was adding to my credibility as an expert in cosmetic dentistry. The other was wanting to go along with the PR and my social media and things that I do to reach the consumers. It just made sense for me to do a book. That really helped, because people do look at you in a different way when you're an author, because not a lot of people know how to do it, or have the bravery, or put the time in to being an author.

When I wrote my first book, it was a big deal to my friends, family, and even patients and people who never met me, because they just don't really write books. There's still not a lot of books on consumer dentistry. There are a lot of dentists who write technical books for other dentists, but it was definitely something that was different for a general practitioner to write for consumers.

Sandi: I don't know if this is related at all to your book or not, but you've had some pretty famous clients.

Catrise: I have had some famous clients.

Sandi: You've been immortalized in song.

Catrise: I've been immortalized in song, and that girl, she's gone to another level. It's just amazing to see her journey. I'm very proud.

Sandi: For the transcription, we're talking about Cardi B.

Catrise: Cardi B, who really just went, it's a Cinderella rags to riches story with her, and her smile transformation had a big part to do with it. Most importantly, she has inspired so many people who would have never called me to call me to see how they can improve their smiles and their lives. I talk in my book, especially *Five Steps to the Hollywood A-List Smile*, I always reference who got teeth whitening. It helps when you can identify that someone whom you admire in entertainment has gone through what you're maybe considering going through. I always reference celebrity in my books, because it also makes it entertaining, because dentistry can be boring.

Sandi: How did you get connected with her? How did she end up coming to you?

Catrise: A couple things happened. She was on a reality TV show, *Love and Hip-Hop*. It's on VH1. I think it's the #1 show on VH1. The producer and creator of that show had been a client of mine, and a friend of mine, for many years. The first season she was getting ridiculed very badly on social media, and then the media, about her smile. I was like, I would love to work with her.

The producer, her name is Mona Scott Young. Mona Scott Young had a wedding anniversary in New Orleans, which I was invited to, and I hap-

70

pened to meet and sit with and get to know one of her producers. The producer needed a smile makeover, and we made a deal that if I do her smile makeover that she would let me videotape her whole procedure, because she actually needed a smile makeover pretty badly. She would let me videotape her getting her smile makeover, and we would use that as a demo reel to pitch for TV shows.

We did the makeover. It was fantastic. Tear-jerking. Everybody loved it. She did a great job with the video. I did not want to send the video to Mona, because I never like to take advantage or assume that my friends will help me. I actually gave her permission to send it to everybody but Mona, and she went behind my back and sent it to her anyway. Out of nowhere, I got a call from her, and she was like, I got Cardi B, who needs a smile makeover. At the time, Cardi B was just a girl on a reality TV show who had a big personality and a terrible smile. I just saw this opportunity to really highlight the work that I do with cosmetic dentistry.

When I got that call from Mona, it was a no-brainer. I took her on as a client. She let me videotape the entire smile makeover too. I have from start to finish, the whole procedure, videotaped, and that was very nice of her. I think one day soon I will get that edited and kind of do the "Behind the

Bodak Yellow Smile" or something like that, so people can see that whole thing transpiring, and see her smile story.

That's how it happened. I took a chance and did a smile makeover on a producer, who put the video together and sent it out. It got into the right hands, and I got the right referral. It's been history ever since.

Sandi: That was a pretty amazing piece TMZ did.

Catrise: Yes. That was totally unexpected, and I didn't realize that TMZ, they feed all the rest of the media outlets. It turned into *Billboard*, and all kinds of magazines picked it up. It was amazing. That was very helpful.

That story dropped when *Bodak Yellow* went #1, and then I saw another surge on Friday, when her album released. It's like every time that she wins or she drops something, my stock goes up too. It's pretty incredible. It's been a great ride.

Sandi: Back to your book, I want to know more about doors that have been opened with having the book. Has it helped you get the media bookings?

Catrise: Yes. Definitely to get on TV it has been extremely helpful. With my book tour with *Get Smiled*, I just pulled out the thing that I know that people in my office ask me the most, which is about teeth whitening, and really pitched that to the media. The fact that I had the book was definitely a factor from the TV appearances that I secured, from *ABC Chicago* to *Good Day New Mexico* to *Good Morning Reno*. Very instrumental. My book was advertised. I can't say I made thousands of dollars in sales, but it's definitely a distinguishing factor in whether you may get booked or not. I am looking forward to releasing this next book and doing another summer media tour.

Sandi: Talking about the writing process and the publishing process, what would you say was the hardest part or the biggest challenge of it?

Catrise: Just squeezing it into your daily life.

Sandi: What was your secret to making that happen?

Catrise: I don't sleep. I require very little sleep, maybe like four hours a day. It's going to catch up to me at some point. But that was the biggest challenge, just after working, I work 10 or 12 hours a day, and then coming home and putting it together was the hardest part. For *Get Smiled*, finding the editors and some of the experts to finalize and make sure that it all came together was a little challenging. Getting the right team. When you find the right team, you want to stick with them and continue on. The last book I did that, and I think you even stepped in to help out in the process.

Sandi: Yeah. If you need editors, I have some good editors now.

Catrise: Perfect.

Sandi: Finding time, and then also the editing process and the formatting process were your challenges.

Catrise: Yeah. Just putting that all together, so that it is ready to be uploaded or printed. Also, for me, I include pictures. I think the one thing that I could improve on in the future is making sure that my pictures, if I'm showing cosmetic dentistry per se, that I really get to the point where we take really book-ready pictures. My pictures are a little homemade looking. The graphics and the design of the book I think I can improve on.

Sandi: Did you find that you had to force yourself to get back to task to meet your deadline, or were you just really excited and passionate about it, and it flowed easy?

Catrise: It flowed easily. I feel like I got a rhythm now of how this thing works, and as long as I can find the time, I could really start cranking out more books.

Sandi: You settled on the formula that works for you.

Catrise: Yeah. That frequently asked question thing kind of really helped.

Sandi: That's a really popular way, especially for experts who do books. You do hear the same questions, probably almost every consultation you do.

Catrise: Yeah. And it's the same answer, so why not just put it together in a few chapters? Voila. In your head, you're like it's got to be 100 or 200 pages. It really doesn't have to be. I think that some people feel like they don't have enough content, when they may very well have it.

Sandi: Right. I get that question a lot. How many words does it need to be? What advice do you have for other experts who have been thinking about writing a book or thinking about publishing a book and just haven't made that leap yet?

Catrise: I would highly encourage them to just dedicate some time to do it. It's not that hard, especially if you consider the formula that I and, like you said, other people have found to do it, just answering questions. With the iPhone and devices where you can dictate, like we're doing right now, it is, I think, super easier now than ever. I know somebody said they do it on Garage Band, or whatever device that you have where you can just speak it, especially if you're just answering questions, and you've got to put some filler material in. It really doesn't have to take a lot of the time that you think it would.

If you just really think that you can't do it, my first book I definitely had a ghostwriter, and I found that person, I think, on Elance, and got some help. I think I was super busy at the time, and found the right writer who could think and talk in my voice, and that worked. Costs you a little bit more money, but I got the book done. There are options out there, if you just don't think you have time.

Just do it. It's really not that hard. It's not that expensive. Now with Amazon and Kindle, CreateSpace, you can create a book and have it published in no time.

Sandi: Pretty low barrier to entry, for sure. I think you're right. I think a lot of it is just the mental game of no excuses. I'm going to do this, and I'm just going to jump in and make it happen.

Catrise: Yeah. Before where maybe Amazon wasn't as big in the book space, and you were trying to get a deal with a publisher, then you had to put together a proposal. It was just so much involved with trying to get a book deal. Do you know people who are searching for book deals now?

Sandi: I knew a couple. I suspect that ultimately they're going to come back around to the idea of self-publishing. I hope that they will go that route and not get sucked into a hybrid publisher.

Catrise: Yeah. I would never do that again.

Sandi: I think if you can get into a publisher who is going to pay you in advance, that believes so strongly in your book that they're willing to literally put their money behind it, then that's something. Of course, that's the dream, right?

Catrise: Right.

Sandi: I think for most authors the trap that they're falling into is that's what they want, but instead they're going with a hybrid publisher, when really they could self-publish and control all their assets and have the same distribution system.

Catrise: Exactly. I hate it with my hybrid publisher that I had a voice, but at the end of the day, there was some decision-making that I probably wouldn't have done. It wasn't that they put a big PR budget behind me. I still had to promote it. It's kind of like me working with the entertainment industry. I know that even though you have a record deal you have to do a lot of promoting yourself. It's not just going to sell itself because you have a record deal.

Sandi: Right. I imagine there's a lot of similarities in the industries. Is there anything else that you'd like to share, or that I should have asked about but didn't?

Catrise: I think maybe if someone was wondering about the cost, like from start to finish, I would say for each of my self-published books, I may have spent

$500, something like that. Not a lot of money to put it together, especially if you go on Upwork, and you find the right people to help you put it together. It really doesn't have to cost you a lot of money. For $500, that's how much I charge for one teeth whitening procedure. It's definitely worth it. You get a return on the investment if you do it right and you promote it and use it as a tool, the tool that it's meant to be.

Sandi: What website would you like me to direct people to?

Catrise: You could do www.vipsmiles.com.

DAVID LENG
- *10 Laws of Insurance Attraction*

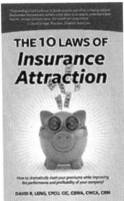
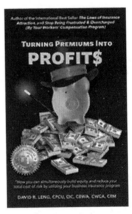

David Leng is a superstar in the business culture, insurance, and risk management fields. As a 30-year veteran of the Risk Management and Insurance industry, he's regarded as one of the brightest minds due to his unique risk profile and culture improvement process. He's also a frequent contributor to several different industry magazines and periodicals. As if that doesn't keep him busy enough, he also volunteers to build sets at the local high school and is an active member of Emmaus and Autism Speaks.

Sandi: You have two books now, right?

David: Three books. I'm on my fourth. The first one is *Stop Being Frustrated and Overcharged,* might be a little long of a title, but it works. It's about helping businesses owners control their worker's compensation insurance and costs. Outside of health insurance, workers' compensation is typically half or more of a business' insurance budget, so slashing the costs of it can have a huge impact on their bottom line. Unfortunately, most business owners believe shopping for premium will reduce their costs, but with workers' compensation, that does not truly work because of all the factors that go into it. The most striking statistic is that the Institute of Work Comp Professionals finds that over 75% of employers believe that they are being overcharged by their workers compensation program.

The second one is the *10 Laws of Insurance Attraction.* Not my favorite title, but it's the only one we could come up with. The world is evolving with the increasing speed and access to information on the internet. However, most business leaders are not aware of how data and analytics are shaping the insurance world today and affecting their insurance premiums. Believe it or not, we have been able to show time and time again that the steps needed to make your business more attractive to insurance companies to earn dramatically lower premiums will actually help increase a business' productivity and profitability. In other words, understanding and improving Business Culture, and implementing a Risk Profile Improvement Program are at the core of this book.

The third one is *Turning Premiums Into Profits*. That's basically an employer's guide to understand alternative risk financing, especially insurance captives. Insurance Captives are the leading way to more effectively reduce their overall insurance costs as well as improve control of their insurance program. As the regulatory and cost structure of self-insurance can be daunting, many businesses are shifting to captives as a way to insure their business, or employee health insurance, in a group with other like-minded and safe businesses, all while building equity rather than just having an expense.

Sandi: Do you have a working title already for your new one, or you're not there yet?

David: I do. It is called *Insured to Fail*.

Sandi: Interesting.

David: That's probably my best title. It actually popped into my head as soon as I started outlining the next subject I wanted to write about. The issue is, even though people buy insurance for their business to pay their claims, they are unaware that when a catastrophe strikes, such as a fire or tornado, that many businesses fail despite being insured. Think about it, how many times have you driven down the street and saw a burned-out building, and then you notice they never reopen? Or they reopen, only to later have a going out of business sale because they couldn't keep the doors open.

I forget the actual statistics. It's in my notes. There was a study done. It's somewhere between 50-60% of businesses that have insurance and suffer a catastrophe either don't reopen or close within three years of reopening – and that statistic does not include events like Katrina. The book is about understanding, from a business owner's perspective, why things went bad, and it typically falls into two categories: Not having the right insurance program, because nobody really knows what insurance they bought until they have a claim, and the other is that they had the wrong plan or process to get themselves back into business. They open up the doors, and then they wonder where the customers are. *If you build it, they will come* does not work in reopening a business all the time.

I've interviewed some business owners that have failed and some that succeeded, but nobody wants to put their name on anything if they failed. It's very difficult. They won't even let me give generalities about the business because they're kind of afraid that someone will figure out who it happened to, so I took it as possibly not wanting to be embarrassed. I get that. But I am trying to figure a way around this issue to make sure that the readers know that these are real stories.

The other angle I am working is I met a guy who has a lot of stories. He worked in the claim department for an errors and omissions liability insurance company that insures insurance agents. He has a ton of stories of individuals who had to resort to suing their insurance agent and insurance company. They suffered a catastrophe and were not being insured properly, or insured as they believed that they were or should have been. In some cases, their lawsuits actually put the insurance agent out of business as the agent was not properly insured too. It's a very interesting concept that should open the eyes of business owners that they should not assume all insurance programs, agents, or companies are the same.

Sandi: Let's talk just for a moment about your actual writing process, how you went from the idea to actually getting your information out on paper.

David: Okay. I had an idea, so attempted to sit down and write, and that did not go anywhere. I then attempted to create an outline and try to write from that, and that was a slow go. After trying to do it for probably 3-4 months I took a pause and a step back. I pretty much said to myself, what are the questions that everybody asks me about worker's compensation? And later, Insurance? Risk Management? Business Culture? Captives? But what are the questions?

It really came does to understand what the questions truly are that employers are asking a solution for. So, where did I get the questions? I diligently focused on compiling information from the business leaders I met for the next two years. I compiled them into my iPad which is full of notes from my risk assessments of businesses, meeting with clients and prospective clients, as well as post workshop survey questions and questions attendees asked when I was speaking at conferences over those two years. Those notes and forms where full of the questions they asked…

I put each question on its own index card, and I had lots and lots of index cards. Then I started clumping them together based on what is the major subject, the major topic, or the major question that they were asking. In some cases, they were redundant. I compiled those over about two weeks working an hour or two each morning.

The really the core questions became the main subject lines or chapters. Under each chapter I put the relating sub questions, and then below each of those, what are the sub-sub questions and continued on like that. It was like building a decision tree under each of the major question or chapter. Then I went back and asked myself what are the key points that you would need to address to answer all of those individual questions, and what case studies do I have in my history where we've addressed or solved those issues? Sometimes I had to make notes and gather data on a case, others just the name of the business was a trigger for the entire story.

Rather than having somebody ask me the questions, I asked the questions to myself and basically recorded it on an audio recorder, either through my portable digital recorder or through my headset on my computer. I created a relationship with InternetTranscribers.com. Normally they charge you a penny a word, and $0.02 a word if you want it grammatically set up in sentences and paragraphs. I've done enough business that they charge me only a penny to put it in sentence format. There are other ones that might be $1 a minute, but this by the word. Every service that was like a $1 or $1.50 a minute might have saved me money, but they came back with just a complete run-on sentence. They sent me back my chapters in some sort of sentence and paragraph format. I had actually done all the preorganization of the structure, and then I recorded it and bundled it up per chapter and sent it down to them as a chapter, so I got them back as a chapter.

After that, I took my notes and wrote the introduction and conclusion. Then I went back and read the entire book. I got rid of redundancies, or if it was something closely related, I inserted a note that referenced another question in another chapter.

Sandi: You also had to do some extra research and go through some compliance checks and things as well, didn't you?

David: When the book was done, because it had not just touched on insurance but also got into the HR world, safety world, compliance world, and stuff like that. I also had three knowledgeable friends read the book. One was the director of the Institute of Work Comp Professionals, one was in the insurance business and one, as I like to say, was an accountant that knew enough to be dangerous. They read it, came back with questions or comments. Then I filled in anything that wasn't clear. Then, once I was done and I had it compiled into a draft of a book, that's when I sent it to an attorney to review it from a compliance standpoint, because of all the HR issues or other compliance issues. Once that got approved, I then went through our own compliance. As I'm a partner in a company that also performs financial services and invests in securities, everything that I do that can be construed as marketing has to go through compliance. That was the last step.

Then I worked with an editor who has a graphics person to put the cover together, clean up all the wording, polish it up and so forth, so it flowed a little bit better. He has a proofreader and people of that sort. Then I pretty much just self-published it with Amazon.

Sandi: Now, working on your fourth book, would you say that the process has become simpler and faster? Your first book you compiled over two years. How long would you say it takes you now?

David: Two years, that was just taking the questions. It took me about 2-3 months to compile all the cards and record and have the draft of the book. The second book I did in about four months. The third book took me about four weeks. By the way, that wasn't my process originally, like I said. The first three chapters took me six weeks, and that's spending an hour or two every day of the week for about two months. Then once I refined the process to how I described it, the remaining nine chapters and intro took me only a month.

Sandi: Wow. Going back when you did your very first book, why did you write it? What was your goal with it?

David: I got challenged by two people who said, "Write a book. You need to write a book." Both from providing what I know to employers, plus better positioning myself in the marketplace, so to speak, as an expert in the field. They literally challenged me to it. The one guy went so far and said, "I'll pay you $500. Write a book." That was a friend of mine dropping the gauntlet to say go write a book.

Sandi: Nice. Your goal with the book was both positioning and client education.

David: As well as to try to open more doors to more businesses as clients, marketing purposes.

Sandi: Where were you before you wrote your book? I don't mean like literally where were you sitting, but I mean in business, in life, what was going on around you at the time?

David: I'm a partner in the financial services firm. I did have a significantly above average size client base. I was actually considered one of the more successful agents in the region. It was about finding another way to meet businesses that didn't necessarily know me. I was already doing workshops in the area, and that was drawing in clients, but the book was a different way to open doors. Since I wrote my first book, I would have to say my client base, has pretty much doubled.

Sandi: That was exactly my next question, the effects of having a book, both on your business and in your life.

David: The biggest way I leveraged it was I go to my raving fan clients. I gave them a copy, and then said, "By the way, who do you know that might benefit from something like this that I could use the book to open the door?"

We sat down. They made some comments to me. I created a note card that said on the front, "*a book just for you...*" with an image of a stack of books on it. Inside I hand wrote the note from their comments. My clients signed the card. They gave me the name and the address, and permission to mail it on their behalf to that prospective business owner. Then a couple days later I called them up and said, "I just was talking to so-and-so. I was taken aback when he told me that he bought one of my books online and sent it to you. I just was curious. Did you get a chance to look at it? Would you like to chat more about it?" It was kind of a complete door opener that wasn't anything like anything else they've ever seen. That's the most effective way of getting new clients.

Sandi: That's brilliant.

David: It was simple. Doesn't cost you very much. Then also my editor, publicist now I guess you could say, did do a speaker kit for me, and we sent it out to about 300 associations nationally and regionally that I know and understand those industries quite well. Now I'm doing speaking engagements. However, as much as that adds to my credibility, when you speak nationally the clients are national, and they're not always anywhere near you. That hasn't necessarily directly developed a lot of business, but it does add a lot of credibility when I approach the local association members that did not attend. That credibility does help open the door. I am only getting about three or four a year that are paid. I also speak to several local associations, but I'm finding they are not always attended by the business owners. They're usually an association that want to educate office staff or HR professionals or something like that. They may or may not always be the right audience. However, It's exposure. It's credibility.

Sandi: I know that one way that some people are using the books, similar to your strategy, although your raving fan actually write the note, that's brilliant. What some people have done as a foot in the door strategy is actually send the book directly from Amazon as a gift with a gift note that you can write on Amazon, so that it could bypass the gatekeeper and get directly to the decision maker, because no gatekeeper is going to open a present.

David: What I could do is literally drop the price that day, that timeframe that I'm on and do that, go in,

I can set up a template so I can do a copy/paste on the note. I would basically just have to pay the shipping charge plus probably the minimum Amazon printing costs, and have the book mailed directly from Amazon.

Sandi: Right. If you have Amazon Prime you wouldn't pay the shipping charge. It would be free shipping. Dropping the price, you could drop the price, but then it kicks it back into the review process, or you could just pay the full price and get your royalty off it.

Going back into writing and publishing, what would you say was hardest part or the biggest challenge of it?

David: Just being focused enough to do it. Actually, probably just starting it.

Sandi: Step 1.

David: Once you get going, you kind of want to finish it. I only have a certain time of the year that I can do it, because from January through end of April I'm volunteering a considerable amount of time with our local high school for the musical. I help design the set, help teach the kids how to build the set pieces, all that kind of good stuff. I do woodworking as a hobby.

Sandi: You said, for other experts, "just do it. Just get

91

started."

David: Yeah. A rolling stone gathers no moss. It's potential versus kinetic energy. You never finish 100% of the projects you never start. That's a twist on hockey's Wayne Gretzky, who says, "You miss 100% of the shots you don't take."

Sandi: That's true. For other experts or thought leaders who are thinking about publishing a book, who have been toying with the idea, what advice do you have for them to get off the fence and to make the process easier?

David: The way I refined my process, it is less difficult. It's not easy, but it's nowhere near as difficult as you think it is. I think you have to understand the fear of the unknown is worse than the known. That's the best I can describe it: is it's not easy, but it's easier than they realize. It's basically carving some time out. I literally carved out, put in my calendar a block of time, an hour or two hours every morning. My employees are like, why are you blocking off every morning? I wouldn't walk into the office until sometimes 8:30 or 9:00 in the morning, when normally I would be there before 8:00. I would get up, and I would work on the book. I didn't go to the gym five days a week. I was down to like two or three. I'd stop at the gym in the evenings on my home instead. You have to do some adjustment.

That's also why I did most of my books in the summer, because in the evening we might be going out. On the weekend I'd be going bicycling in the mountains or kayaking, so I was doing other things to kind of keep busy physically. If I was doing it in the winter, it probably would actually have been health wise as there is less to do in the evenings outside. It does take your focus. With me having a business of almost 100 employees, there's only so much time in the day.

The book writing was only half of it. It probably took me just as long or longer to put together the website, documents, supportive materials, a sequence if they registered the book. All that took probably as long or longer than writing the book. Once again, I was doing it myself. I actually got Adobe Creative Suite, and I used Adobe Muse, and I made my own websites.

Sandi: Having a team behind you can probably shorten a lot of those things, right?

David: Yeah. A team or knowing where to go to get certain things done. On the other hand, I did all that, and from a dollar cost standpoint, between the editor, the graphics person for the cover, prepping and the transcription, I probably didn't even spend $1,000 on the book. It was all the other stuff that it took.

Sandi: What I'm really finding is everybody's process and backend of it is so different. It's fascinating.

David: I know somebody that all they do is help people write books. They basically write them, they publish them, they market them, and you pay well into the five figures to get it done. It's interesting.

Sandi: Is there anything else you'd like to share, or that I should have asked that I didn't?

David: When I go to interview the guy that used to be the errors and ossmisions claims person I was thinking about using just this same process, and then having it transcribed, so I can go straight to editing it to use. I guess that's about it.

Sandi: My last question is what is the website that you would like me to put in the book for people who might be interested in your services, that happen to be in your area?

David: If you want to, I'll give you both of them. The first one you can go based off the first title, www.stopbeingfrustrated.com . It's also called the www.premiumreductioncenter.com . Either way gets there. That is my business site.

If you're going to be a speaker as well, I would recommend a separate speaker website. I didn't do this the first time, so when I went to try to get speaking engagements everyone was directed to the stopbeingfrustrated.com. It was focused towards both employers and business group initially, so it was a little clunky. I set up the one website at one time, and I put everything into it. After going through the attempt to obtain speaking gigs, I then separated the speaking website out, and now I've got www.davidleng.com on the speaker side. Not a perfect site, but that would be a big recommendation. Make sure you have your own speaking website.

It's not just that, but you can repurpose what you write to do other things. I am now in national magazines and articles for employer-focused magazines, and then I have a Press Room on each of those sites, because it works both ways. One to try to work with associations for speaking opportunities, and one to work for employers. You earn more credibility when they see you are published in national magazines. Some periodicals I am published more consistent than others, and because of that I don't put all of them up there.

Sandi: I think being recognized as a regular contributor is very powerful.

David: I have now been published over 28 times in magazines. A couple of them I developed a relationship with, but a couple my editor developed the relationship with. The problem is that sometimes you develop a relationship with a magazine, and then a new editor comes in, and he has his own sources. I lost one national magazine that way. I went from being a contributor three or four times a year, and then they hire a new editor, and I lose the relationship.

Sandi: What about local radio and TV?

David: I haven't done any of that.

Sandi: There's another place you could start sending your books.

David: That's not a bad idea. I didn't think of that. The other interesting part was I have had the newspaper reach out to me.

Sandi: Awesome. That's it. Those are all my questions. I really appreciate you taking the time to speak with me. You were a great interview.

David: I appreciate it.

Sandi: I appreciate it. Thank you very much, especially on such a busy day.

ROBIN RICHTER
– *Golf Course Millionaire*

 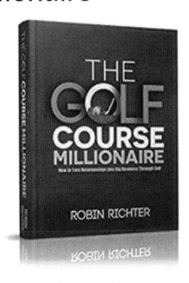

Robin is co-founder and president of Wearable Imaging Inc. a provider of superior advertising specialty products to Fortune 500 and small businesses since 1992. Robin has been playing golf since she was young. She was a golf pro on the tour for two years before joining corporate America. Since then she has integrated her love of the game with her formula for business success. She's also a master networker, and one of those people who just make you feel good when you're around her.

Sandi: My first question is about your writing process, that is how you went from the idea to the written word. How did you go from the blank page to actually having it in hand?

Robin: I started really thinking about writing the book in 2012, and basically the first idea that I had in my head was to outline and make it 18 chapters, with the 19th hole being the 19th chapter. What I did, was I started out with the first hole, but what I found was I was trying to fit a square peg in a round hole, because 19 chapters is a lot in a book that I really only wanted to do 100 to 125 pages. I quickly realized that that probably wasn't the best route, although a lot of the content that I had outlined in the different chapters was still very relevant.

I was kind of just rethinking, based on all the relationships that I had. After consulting with you, you said, you know a lot of people, you should talk about your experiences. I thought maybe I should interview people, and just started writing down names of experts or people I knew who actually did business on the golf course or used golf as a connector to business. I rethought the whole process on how I wanted to do it and started out with just reaching out to several people and coming up with six people to interview. I got the interviews set first.

It wasn't always in an organized fashion, because it was knowing that I wanted to interview people, and that sort of created a life of its own after the interviews actually took place. You know what I'm saying?

Sandi: I want to know more about what happened after the interviews took place.

Robin: I took the conversations that I had with these people and tied it all in, how that similar thing happened to me or whatever. Each person brought life to the book, because they talked about their experiences and their stories. Their stories were exciting and motivating. Although each story was unique, in every case golf was the connector.

I start the book by giving my history, how I learned how to play at the age of nine, and my entire life story that has built up to what I'm doing today, which is Wearable Imaging, my company of 26 years. Selling promotional products, but in a very different, unique creative way. Using golf still, to this day, to create relationships and build my business. I have some really interesting parts of my life, and I've shared all that. How my dad passed away, and how I took over the business on my own. Then my husband ended up starting to work in the business, and how I've grown the business to this day.

When I was younger, I thought I was going to play professional golf. That was it. However, I realized that I didn't want to be out there competing and being on my own. I was more a team player. My whole story evolved in the book, and I give all kinds of tips. Even if you don't play, here's how you can incorporate the game of golf into your business. After reading this book, you may be inspired to play. Like you, Sandi.

Sandi: That's right. Yeah.

Robin: If you do play, I answer how can you utilize golf to build your business and certain ways of getting involved. It's just really taken on a life of its own. It's just been so exciting. It's only been about a month since it's published, and it's crazy. You want me to talk about the video that I did?

Sandi: Hold onto that one for just a second, because I want to know more about these interviews that you did. Did you know everybody that you interviewed, or was there anybody that you reached out to that you had never met before?

Robin: I knew five out of the six people. I took two famous people whom I think everybody would know, or if they didn't they would Google them and quickly enough know. Hiram Smith, who is one of the co-founders of Franklin Covey. I met him about six years ago, had the privilege of playing golf with him. Again, I stood out from several hundred people, because I play golf. We had that connection. To get to know him and him get to know me over a five-hour round was amazing. I believe that reaching out to him years later to ask him to interview, he was thrilled. He was so thrilled, and I'm thinking this is such a famous guy, he's going to say no. Sure enough, he agreed.

The other famous person was Betsy King, and she's 34-time LPGA hall of famer, won over 34 tournaments on the LPGA tour. Was the president of the Solheim Cup, very well-known person, and just has a fascinating story, how she ties her charity, Golf for Africa, that she's passionate about, into all the connections that she has through golf. She's made over $9 million with the charity. I think she founded it in 2008. I can't remember. You'll have to look in my book.

Then just a few other friends and people whom I know who are very successful in business, because of the game of golf. One gentleman who I did not know was Robert Ford. I was given his name through somebody else who was helping me edit the book. She knew that he had a very successful career and that he was a big golfer and had some amazing stories. He's a big IT executive and worked for Virgin Records. He told how he learned to play and what it's done for his career and stuff. It was just really interesting. At the end of the conversation, it was like we've got to play. I want to play. Again, it's just that connection. Very smart, interesting guy.

Sandi: So, even somebody who didn't know you was very receptive to your request for an interview.

Robin: Very much so, which is so cool. Not one of the six people whom I talked to turned me down. They were actually very thrilled. I think it's always fun when you talk about stories of when you were a kid, and it makes you feel good to talk about just all these cool things that maybe not everybody knows. You don't just sit around and talk about that kind of stuff. It's usually what's going on day to day in your life. It's kind of fun to reminisce. I think they really enjoyed sharing part of their lives with me, and I was honored. For each one of them, I signed the book, and I really let them know how appreciative I was for them contributing to this amazing journey and sent it to them in the mail. They all were just very touched.

Sandi: You did these interviews, and then what? Did you listen to the interview and transcribe it yourself?

Robin: I signed up for FreeConferenceCall.com. Anybody can do it. You just have the call-in number with the access code. You push record. You record the conversation. What I did was I sent them the questions ahead of time and said, feel free to ad-lib. This is not a formal thing. This is just a general guideline of the questions I'm going to ask, because I asked different questions for every person. Some of them were similar. Some of them were different, based on their background and experience. Then you send the recording to somebody to transcribe it. In my case, I used Rev.com. Then they have a live person who transcribes the call, and they send it back to you. I liked it, because they wouldn't put in all the 'ums' or 'ahs' or 'you knows.' They would delete all that. It came back pretty clean.

Then Katie, one of my editors, I sent it to her. Then we would work on it together. She would do the pre-editing and try to get it more into the story format, and then I would interject, if I thought I should really expand on this part. Then we did that. Just to have the recordings, written and voice, were invaluable, especially Hiram Smith. His story is just crazy, so interesting. It was so fun. I think he was so excited to share. Not anybody just sits down with him and says, tell me about when you started learning to play golf. People just don't do that. I think it just sparked this light in him. He was so excited. He called me twice after he read it, and then he called me again and just said, I'm so excited. It made me cry. I was so excited.

Sandi: You did your interviews. You got them transcribed. You had the help of an editor. Then, obviously, through the technical stuff, formatting and all of that. Why did you write your book?

Robin: I've been paying golf for 50 years, and I feel like I've had so many amazing things happen to me, and it's all because of this game. You could be just talking about it, and there's just this connection between two people. I just felt so passionate about it that I really wanted to share my stories with other people, in hopes that it would break down the walls of intimidation to people that say, I can't play. Either it's too expensive, or I'm not good enough. That's why they have handicaps, #1. You play with people who are of your own caliber. I feel like after reading my books, and you can attest, do you feel more comfortable? I really think I can go out and do this. You don't even have to be coordinated. You don't have to be smart. You don't have to have a ton of time. I wanted to break down those walls of intimidation. I also wanted to maybe inspire the person who does play to have more of a purpose that this could really help build my business, especially if you're an entrepreneur and you're in sales.

I wanted to kind of leave a legacy for my son as well, so he always knows. His children, grandchildren, here's a piece of your grandmother. It's kind of cool. It's not often that we talk about our lives. Tell me about your life story. What was really interesting was my father-in-law read the book, and later told me, I never knew that about you. I'm really sorry that that happened to you in your life.

You know what, everything that happens to us makes you who we are today, makes us stronger, makes us better. I'm not sorry for anything.

Sandi: Where were you before writing your book? I don't mean physically. I was sitting in my living room. I mean, in your business, in your life, what was going on around you before you wrote the book?

Robin: I've been talking about writing my book since 2012. You get to a point where you're in Mastermind groups, I have a business coach, and we talk about our goals. This year, these are my business goals. These are my personal goals. Writing a book was always on my list. Never got crossed off. Finally, my coach said to me, probably back in October of 2017, I'm really tired of you talking about this. That's what a coach is for. I finally just said, I'm tired of talking about it too. I'm tired of hearing myself. I'm just going to do it. I buckled down and went to the course for three days and did the whole thing. Then you commit to a deadline. Somehow, you have to get it done. I'm just that type of person. If you put a deadline in front of me, I'm going to get it done. I'm not going to tell the world I'm doing something and let all of them down, including myself. That was huge for me. Kind of like in college, when you go 'my final is this.' Then you start buckling down. You've got to study. You've got to do it.

I think what I learned in this process, and what I learned about everything in business, there is no time. There is no perfect time. Never a perfect time. You just have to do it.

Sandi: Kind of like having a baby.

Robin: Yeah. I've used that example. It's like birthing a child. It's never been so hard to do this whole project, but I have my book sitting here in front of me talking to you. I just get this feeling of gratification. I feel like I'm so proud of myself that I finally did this. It was so hard, but so gratifying. I ended my work day at 6:00, and I was working on it until 9:00 or 10:00, or whatever. You take your Saturdays and your Sundays, and you just do it. That's what you have to do. Once it's done, it's like a blink of an eye. It's done. Time just goes by so fast. I still sometimes look at this, and I go, I can't believe I did this. You know? I really do.

Sandi: Before you wrote your book, you already had a business. You already had an incredible social circle.

Robin: Yes. I have a successful promotional advertising business of 26 years, which I'm super proud of, but there are a lot of people in my space, and the third reason I wanted to write this book, I talked about the two, in my business we have promotional items that have logos on there, I do what they call self-promos. I put my Wearable Imaging logo on mugs and pens and cool things that I see that come out. I'm always doing fun, unique things, where everybody will say, that's so cool. Where'd you get it? I want it. That's kind of my whole drive. I thought, what if I incorporated my business throughout this book, and I utilized it to give away as a promotional item to potential new clients? How is that going to set myself apart from all the other people in my space? Who writes a book? Not everybody who's in this industry. I don't know of anybody in this industry, off the top of my head, I'm sure there are a lot, that have written a book. I can talk about what it's done for me so far.

Sandi: That is my next question, in fact, what the effect of having that book has been. I know that things started happening even before it was done, right?

Robin: Yeah. Absolutely. We designed the cover during that period in December, so now you have the cover, and you can do all kinds of things with it. We did a lot of social media, like pre-launching type stuff and talking about the process or when it's coming out, that kind of thing. I have a social media person who did a whole series of things to pre-launch.

I saw someone post this video of her sitting in her office and opening up her book for the first time and seeing and feeling the actual cover. I literally stopped, turned up the volume, and watched that video of her. It just really brought tears to my eyes. I was in that course with her, and I personally know her, so I was like that is so cool. I was so happy for her.

A few weeks later, I got this idea. I told Emily, my gal, we need to do this too. She said, yes, we need to get you more on video and really post that. I was thinking, how am I going to do this? Where am I going to do this? It wasn't scripted or anything, by any means, because that's not me. I'm more a shy, behind the scene kind of person. When you told me the book was ready, I got so excited, and then you told me, we did a matte cover, I hope you like it. I was really excited. I didn't want to wait to order the author's copy. I went onto Amazon Prime and ordered it and got it in two days. I paid full price.

So, I got it. This is funny, because I got it on a Wednesday. I had a baseball cap on, coming from my son's baseball game. I'm like, I can't video now. I look terrible. What am I going to do? All of a sudden, it came to me. I'm playing in a golf tournament on Friday. I'm going to do it on Friday. I was like a kid in a candy store at Christmas, or whatever, that I can't open this until Friday, until we actually go out on the golf course and we videotape.

I had this envelope just sitting there staring at me for two days. Then my friend, who was one of the people that I happened to be playing with, I asked, can you video me? Nothing was scripted. She bought a bottle of champagne, so we celebrated, but I didn't know how this was going to go. I said, just video me. I'm going to open this envelope, and let's just video. It became so emotional and just crazy. I didn't know how I was going to feel, and when I opened it I just started to cry. I don't know.

Sandi: It was very moving.

Robin: Thank you. Right now, it has over 12,000 views, and it's crazy. I've had people reach out to me, like I was so inspired. I went and bought your book, or I downloaded your book. Will you please sign it? I mean, on and on and on. I made sure that personally I thanked every single person. Every day I was having to answer 25, 30, crazy. It was just such a cool moment that I'll always have on video. It comes from the heart.

Continuing, what am I doing, I took the back of my Wearable Imaging business card and put a picture of my book on there, and I created a QR code that you can actually click on that, and it goes right to Amazon. You can order my book. I also put on my emails, like the bottom of the Wearable Imaging email, it says #1 bestselling author of *The Golf Course Millionaire: How to turn Relationships into Big Business Through Golf.* Again, there's a picture of my book, and actually a mug that I created, because I'm in the business. I put a picture of my book on a coffee mug. We collaged that together, and again there's a link to go into Amazon to purchase the book. We're doing a lot of other promoting, the keyword, utilizing the keywords to promote the book.

I've been asked to do book signings. I just did a huge presentation with Honda of America. Before I even got started with the presentation, there were 20 people in the room. I gave my book out to everybody and talked a little bit about it and how it incorporated business and promotional whatever. It was literally a game changer. I walked out of that room getting two huge deals.

One guy, he walks out of the room. He had his arms crossed the whole time, and I thought he's so not interested. Walks out of the room, and he goes, I'm going to read your book. I was checking you out on Amazon, and you've got great reviews. You got five-star reviews. I'm going to read your book. Would you sign it for me? I'm like, of course. It was just so funny. This guy, I'm thinking he's not interested, he actually was very impressed.

Sandi: What other opportunities have come to you because of the book?

110

Robin: I have a book signing coming up at the WBENC conference in Detroit. I've been asked to come to one of my client's booths and sign books and promote it, in about a month. I've been asked a couple of times already to be interviewed. I've been asked to go onto two podcasts. I'm more on the shy side, so I'm not as comfortable doing a lot of this yet, but I'm pushing out of my comfort zone. You have to get out of your comfort zone and do it. It's only been three weeks. I have a lot of people talking to me about it and congratulating me, just coming out of the woodwork. How did you do that? You're so busy. How did you fit that in? I can't even believe, you're Superwoman. That's what I'm hearing. You just do it.

Sandi: It's only been three weeks? It feels like it was so long ago already.

Robin: Believe me, I know. It certainly does.

Sandi: These media appearances are just starting to materialize. The book also helped you deepen relationships with some of the people you interviewed, right? You were saying that you talked to Hiram multiple times now.

Robin: Yeah. I felt like they were really doing me a favor, but what I'm realizing is that I really did them a favor, and not knowing that, but how appreciative they've been to me. Donna Hoffman, *Woman on Course*, she's doing a big signature event coming up in July, and she wants me to do a book signing and really promote the book. I think it's just the tip of the iceberg, to be honest, because my hope is that maybe I can get this into some of the pro shops, some of the golf chains, as resale. Even my hairdresser is putting it in her salon, because people are saying, my husband plays. It's crazy. I really am so proud of the cover and so proud of the way it turned out.

Sandi: I can't wait to hear what comes next for you. Every day you're getting new opportunities. If this is only three weeks in, I can't wait to see what's coming up.

Robin: Me too.

Sandi: What was the hardest part and the biggest challenge of the writing and publishing process? You took this huge bite. You made this giant commitment by doing a pre-release, and then you're kind of up against the wall, and you've got to make it happen. Let's talk about the hardship part of it.

Robin: Well, you're like, seriously? I just committed to this? I have the general premise of what I wanted to do, but I really had no idea how it was all going to come together. I really didn't. I think that's the biggest misnomer with people. You don't just have to have it all together. It's a process, and you figure it out as you go. Katie was extremely helpful in laying out for me the outline. Here's where we're at. This is what we need to finish. Really writing down the layout, having it written out, because I'm very visual. It's like, these are the holes that need to be filled in. You need to finish the forward, or you need to finish your story.

As I thought of things that I wanted to add, I talked into Rev, saying this is help filling in Chapter 4. Then it would spit it out, rather than me typing. I don't think that there was any part of this book that was hand typed by me. It was all dictated. I think, again, people are going to probably be very shocked to hear that. You think that you're writing a book sitting down at a computer and typing away, but that's just not the way it is. Rev, I think that's the best thing since sliced bread. I'm not kidding.

I drive down to San Diego a lot. I remember the drives, and I remember just driving along the ocean and talking about parts of the book. It was very emotional, talking about my dad and my mentor, Bud. They're both gone. You start crying and stuff. It's so much easier for me to talk about something than to type it, because I feel the emotion came out better that way. I would strongly urge people to use Rev.com. I think, it's like a puzzle. It's like when you shoot a movie, sometimes you shoot the ending first. It's kind of like that. It's all over the place, and you're trying to put it together where it kind of all fits and it all flows. That was probably the biggest challenge. What do we do with this? What do we do with that? We can insert it into this chapter, because this is talking about golf tournaments, or whatever it was.

I think one of the other things that was helpful, and that I got a lot of positive feedback from, was using pictures. When I talked about each one of these people who I interviewed, I showed a picture of either myself with them or found a good photo of them and put that in there. Then when I'm talking about my dad, I have pictures. Talked about my hole-in-one, I have pictures.

You helped me with the gallery and all of that in the back. You helped me put a lot of, the forward, where does that go? Where does the glossary go? You really helped me lay out the chapters. As I said before, and I'm going to say this because we're being recorded now, I don't think that I could have done this without you. I'm so grateful to you and for finding the right person to help me complete it. You brought it to completion, and I so thank you for that.

Sandi: You're too kind. It was my pleasure. I remember, as we were going through it, it wasn't without its stress. It is a huge giant elephant that you choose to eat. You did ultimately decide to push back for an extra month. Tell me a little bit more about what was going through your

114

mind when you were getting overwhelmed with it and how you pushed through it.

Robin: I went into the back end of KDP, and I started researching, can you extend your deadline? It did say yes. I felt like I was almost to the 30 day, and I wasn't ready. I didn't want to put something out that I didn't feel so comfortable with. I knew that if I had 30 more days it would be exactly what I wanted. I was almost there, but I didn't want to rush it. Then when I reached out to you and said, I know Amazon says you can do this, but what are the ramifications? Really, what you told me, which was so reassuring, was the only thing you can't do is publish a book in the next year. We knew that wasn't a problem. Really, that was the only downfall. I was like, I don't know if I'll ever write a book again. Who knows? Never say never.

Sandi: What advice do you have for other experts who, like you, have been thinking about it for a long time, but for whatever reason can't find the time or whatever, or are intimidated by the process? Who knows what's holding them back?

Robin: We all know the famous Nike tagline. Just do it. There never is a right time. You just have to do it. It's making the commitment, whether it's working with you or taking a course or whatever, but I strongly would recommend working with you. You take that step, and you commit.

I'm going to do this. Then you hire the right people. You have to have a team around you. You have to have a designer. You have to have an editor. You have to have a proofreader. You have to have somebody to put it into the right format, who knows whether it's the KDP route or the CreateSpace route or however you're going to go. You have to align yourself with the people who know what they're doing. Don't try to do it on your own. That's my advice. Don't try to do it on your own. You'll waste so much time and so much money. Find the right people. I knew the right people, didn't I?

Sandi: You did. You definitely did.

Robin: It took me more time and money to find you, and, like I said, I'm grateful to you. It was a journey. I can look back and give people advice and probably save them twice as much money and twice as much time by knowing the right people to go to. That's huge. Isn't it? It's not sometimes what you know, it's who you know.

Sandi: For sure. You're either going to put in money or time.

Robin: Absolutely.

Sandi: Is there anything else you'd like to share or any questions that I should have asked, but I didn't?

116

Robin: I think that a lot of people say, I could never do this, and I'm here to say that if I can do it, you can do it. People are like, I had no idea that you're a writer or an author or this or that. You don't have to be, because there are so many amazing people and that's what they do. They can help you bring it out in you. That's really what Katie did for me, you did for me. You maybe have all this stuff inside you that you want to share, but you don't know how. I think aligning yourself with the right people, it's kind of like if you don't know how to dress. You have somebody that dresses you. It's you, but you just happen to have this adorable outfit on, and you look amazing. You feel so good about yourself. It's kind of the same thing. This book is me, but it's better than what I could have ever done, because of the help and the support that I had around me. Does that make sense?

My family is so over the moon proud of me. That's what's cool. You have so many people coming out of the woodwork saying, I saw you on Facebook, that is so awesome. I'm so proud of you. How did you find time to do it? I said, I didn't. I just made it happen. It's like anything in life. When tragedy happens, you say, how did this person go through it? They say, I just did, because I had to. I think when you're given a deadline, and you put it out there to the world, that's the best part, because you're scared half to death. That motivation is what got me through it. I'm like, I'm not going to let these people down, or myself. I'm so proud of myself and so happy and so thankful. It's just an amazing feeling that I can't even describe. A big thanks to you.

Sandi: My pleasure. I really can't wait to see all the amazing things that are opening up for you and that will be happening to you as you keep taking advantage of all these opportunities that present themselves.

Robin: Thank you so much. Me too. I'm looking forward to it. I am. That's what is so cool. You just don't know what tomorrow is going to bring or who's going to read your book and be inspired. That's what you want. You want people to go, I read your book, and I was really inspired. I want to grow my business. I want to learn to play. Now golf is not as intimidating as I thought. You inspire me. You want to inspire people.

Website: www.wearableimaging.com

KEVIN FREAM
– *Streamlining Technology*

Kevin is CEO of Matrixforce and brings 25 years as a cyber security advisor to prospective customers. He specializes in helping business owners and leadership teams reduce technological complexity and avoid risk, paying special attention to current compliance penalties that impact the viability of nearly every business. He specializes in mid-sized businesses of $5 million to $150 million in revenue. As you can imagine, this keeps him incredibly busy, and yet he still found time to write his books.

Sandi: My first question is about your writing process. How did you go from the idea of having a book to the written word? You were just telling me that you're going to do another book, and that you think you can bang it out in a week or so. I'd love to hear more about both the process of your last book and how you have the next book organized in your mind to be able to knock it out so quickly.

Kevin: Right. I'm a student of what people do. I find mentors and go after that. There's usually a business reason that pushed it. In 2009, our company had been in business 30 years, and we had a start-up come along. They were just killing the market. They had a tv commercial, and they had this website that was ranking everywhere. They did press releases and that kind of stuff. I was like, we have a website. Been there a long time. What is the difference? They had started doing some very simple marketing, but one of the things that they had started but not done very well was blogging. In 2009 I started down the blogging road.

Fast forward to today, some of the people are the Brian Harris and the Brian Deans of the SEO world, and since 2009 that's really been my focus, search engine marketing and all the stuff around it. I told you this story about Easy Prey. I had this great compilation book with 19 other authors, and it went #1 bestseller in cybersecurity and solidified my reputation in cybersecurity. Even though I have 25 years, suddenly your reputation is there.

People started saying, Kevin, you didn't write all of that book. You only wrote a chapter. I used my blog for objection handling, and I purposely have what I call a divergent blog formula. The whole premise of our business, and also the same thing as our blog, is to do something that's unexpected. The ways most people approach things are kind of normal and boring, and they don't ever get anywhere. I had 10 years' worth of content that was using this kind of approach. If you have a picture, it's an unusual picture. Always have a video.

You start with a hook, and it may have a celebrity catch or an interesting opening line or an interesting place. Then telling a few stories with it. That became powerful, as far as if you're educating people and entertaining them, and you're not really talking about your company, but you have an eBook that has an offer with it. It all became very powerful.

I did *Streamlining Technology* in three days, because I had basically almost 10 years' worth of content to pick and choose from that was in a ready format. There's not another #1 bestselling managing IT services book out there. I needed it for Harvard, but it also is a cornerstone part of what we call our shock and awe box, if you know what that is.

Sandi: I do know what it is, but for the benefit of the transcriptionist, if you wouldn't mind going into more detail about your shock and awe box and what you do with it.

Kevin: Sure. The shock and awe box is if you've investigated and researched, and you have your dream clients that would like to get, you get a list together, and then the adage is the average salesman spends a buck on a folder and some flyers about their company and products, whereas if you can put a shock and awe box together that has a #1 bestselling book and it has a DVD or thumb drive with your stories at NASDAQ and Harvard and Microsoft and Coca-Cola, and then you have eBooks about the definitive trusted advisor guide and how not using vetted IT support is willful neglect. If you have the service provider advisory that talks about how we do things versus the common stuff in the industry and how you should pick people that match with what you're trying to do in your business, really strong content things that provide some value right out of the gate.

We spend $150 on the stuff that's in the box, because there might be a nice phone or tablet charger, pen, and a mousepad and some other stuff with it, and several other pieces of material that we put together that are really strong content. For that $150 that we may spend on them, our average contract is somewhere around $300,000 over three years.

Sandi: That's a great investment.

Kevin: Is it worth it to do that? Yeah. Is it worth it to invest in and have strong content and do books and push them to #1 bestseller? Yes. All of that just builds credibility and shows who you are. You're a much different animal in the marketplace.

Sandi: What a great idea. Back to your writing process for a moment. That you were able to repurpose content that you had out there in other formats is fantastic, and a great way to streamline it and do it quickly. Let's talk about for a moment when you're sitting down to write a blog post. A lot of people get very overwhelmed by the blank page or the blank screen, if you will. Do you have any little tricks or tips or a process that you go through when you're sitting down to write one of your posts that help you get over the blank screen?

Kevin: Sure. Every day we write things that we run across in our business, and we have a topic, a list of ideas. Usually there's stuff that comes up.. Since we do business blogging, we tend to do our posts based around a campaign. For instance, right now the big thing is we have a new trademark on Vetted IT Support that has just been published. Most people don't know what Vetted IT Support is, so we get things like, who decides who's vetted? Is that just you, you made this up in some clever marketing? We have a post that talks about how government authorities require this, and the industry requires this now, because of these regulations. Everybody is underneath it, in case you don't know why. We kind of go through and answer those.

We have more topics than we can usually do, and we generally have four main categories that we do around our blog. We'll simply do round robin and say, we did one on cybersecurity. It's time to do one on disaster recovery and online backup. We did one on cloud computing, and we need to do one on the business bangs with technology. We'll kind of go back and forth.

We pretty much have the divergent blog post formula. It's always not about a product or not about our company. It's usually we tell a story, and the story opens up with a hook, and that hook is usually around some kind of celebrity attach or a place. That's where we start off first. The other real big component is everybody that's doing blogging tells the how and what. We like to try to tell the why. The good analogy is everybody in our business tells the what. They say, we do IT support,

124

and that's what we do. How we do it is we have these great people, and they're all certified. We have lots of them. Doggone it, people like us. Would you like to get some IT support? It's the same thing over and over.

Whereas we start different. It's kind of similar to the Apple thing. We say, we believe most things in business and technology are broken and not done in a way to get results. We'll usually do the opposite. We streamline technology to reduce what you have, reduce the risks, reduce the complexity. It's less for you to buy and less for you to own. We do Vetted IT Support. We're a C corp. We have intellectual property. Our specialty is Microsoft Cloud and security. We're published authorities, and here are our executive summaries from all our regulation compliance, including our Delta methodology, that's the only patented methodology in the world to get 40,000 projects done effectively and on time in the last 40 years. Would you like to do IT support with us?

It's a different thing, because I started with the why and why it was so much different. We try to do that. It's very difficult to kind of get the concept, but if you start off with the why, all these motivations about selling, you go away from that, about your selling your company and that kind of stuff. That's a big part of it.

Then we have some basic rules, because of having the background of doing the search engine marketing. Most of that is also not true of everything they tell you. Post every day or whatever, have a schedule and research this, and put it everywhere, and you'll be fine. We have some rules about we're not fake news. Whatever your politics are, we usually have a link to a reputable source of where this information came from. We have a link to another post that's related.

We're focused on conversion, so we have a call to action with everything we have. It may be here's the definitive Trusted Advisor guide, and at the end of it there's a no cost obligation to get a cybersecurity risk assessment. It outlines what that is. Even if you don't do business with us, you have a great asset, and you know what you can do from there. Those are the high levels that we hit, basically though four of five real big things.

The board says that I'm gifted. I'm not sure if I believe that or not, as far as writing.

Sandi: I believe it.

Kevin: I may not have helped you much, but that's my process.

Sandi: No, that's great. With your first book, why did you write it?

126

Kevin: The first book was a compilation with other authors. I wasn't on the board, and it's like I've been doing this for 8 or 9 years, but I had heard that message about being an author and writing books you're never going to make money on the books. Robin Robbins in our industry came along and told the story very well if you become a bestselling author, that's something they can never take away from you. You can be part of the national bestselling authors association, and here are all the other things that you can go with it. Everybody talks about writing a book, but they don't ever do it. Oh by the way, it's not as much about doing the book. It's just like everything else in your business, it's to prove that you can actually deliver on what you say. It adds a piece of legitimacy to it, and so that's why I did the first one with *Easy Prey*.

The second one, like I said, everyone said, you didn't write that one, so I did *Streamlining Technology* immediately and had it ready for Harvard.

Sandi: Focusing on *Streamlining Technology*, since that is your solo book, it was really a status builder, right?

Kevin: Status building. Let's talk about hard dollars, the first book, Easy Prey, it cost me about $7,000, which made me kind of angry actually. I knew I had to get in the game and learn. They had a ghostwriter for everybody, and it turned out that

127

for everybody else he wrote their chapter. He didn't know anything about cybersecurity. I wrote. 2,000 words is not a big deal. I wrote things in, and also I looked at the previous books that they did, and everybody was writing all the same things. I talked about business things, and I gave five really good ideas that nobody had in the other chapters..

Then it's like, there's this free giveaway, and then we've got to have this big push at the end. It took six months, and I couldn't figure out. I did my chapter in three days and talked to this guy for two hours, because he needed to fill the time, apparently, to find out who I was, because I had already written all the content. Then we did this stuff.

It came together. We did the push at the end. Because there were so many companies involved and everybody was doing this great giveaway, it went to #1 bestseller. I spent $7,000 on the book. I put another $5,000, so $12,000 total for let's pick the right box. We got this slick box for our shock and awe, and then put all the other content with it. Here's the chargers and the really nice pen and all the other kind of stuff and the content. I spent $12,000 on that, and then within the next three months I sold half a million dollars in recurring revenue on that.

So, I said, this book thing is probably a pretty good deal. I did combine it with a shock and awe concept and some other stuff with it. *Streamlining Technology*, it just kind of adds greatly to the status. I'm a big believer in none of this stuff really stands alone either. Doing tv and some of the great talks at the really renowned venues, it makes a great story.

Sandi: Would you be able to address the effects of having a book? I know that it's only one piece of your shock and awe package, so it might be difficult to single it out. Has it changed your business and your life to have your book, or books?

Kevin: It's going from nobody to somebody. I mean, you have a book? The one thing that Robin Robbins and a lot of folks teach you is your book is now your business card. They see a book with your face on it when you're talking to a client in the restaurant, that's what the waiter will say, you're somebody. You got your picture on your book. You see that? It's even like this morning. I was introduced to somebody, and it's like, you have a card? We're at the gym, but I went out, and I carry a box of books in the trunk and took him back a book. It was $20 hardcover or whatever, but it's an impression. It's you're standing out differently. You're different in front of clients, and people that you run across. That's the impact it's had for me.

Sandi: Nice. Helping you land half a million dollars of business is no small thing either. That's pretty amazing.

Kevin: Right. We're going to use that for quite some time.

Sandi: What would you say was the hardest part or the biggest challenge of the writing and publishing process?

Kevin: I didn't struggle with the content. I know a lot of people do. The cover was a real challenge, and just some of the little rules. The images inside your book aren't clear enough. You need to make them sharper. It was the same thing on the cover. CreateSpace has this cover creator, but it's really clunky. You're pretty limited. I found out pretty quickly that I didn't like any of the templates, but I could pick a couple where I could put in my own image for the cover, and then they had a template for the back, and you could pick your color and then type in the what the back was. That wasn't too bad, except for they had really stringent rules on the image.

Then it was diving into cover design. There are people who specialize in cover design. It's one of those things you go back to people like yourself say, you need to go to Amazon, or your favorite heroes of authors, and go and look at their covers and emulate that. That sounds easy, but it's really not.

My first cover on *Streamlining Technology* was really basic, and I did that for two reasons. One is because I didn't know what the hell I was doing, and I needed to get a cover out real quick. Two, *Streamlining Technology* is all about let's not buy more stuff and just keep growing. It's truly about minimalism. Again, less to buy is less to support, and it's less to attack. So, that's why I did it.

Sandi: I often will direct my authors to 99 Designs to do the cover, because that way you can initiate a contest and have graphic designers bidding for your work by showing you samples of what they would do for you and what they can do with your cover with the specifications that you put out there. You're right. The cover is so personal, and so important, because a lot of people may not actually read the book. They're just going to literally take it at face value. That cover can be everything and can be one of the hardest things to get right. That's definitely a struggle.

Kevin: With my background, I'm kind of a do-it-yourself guy, when I can be. I figured I'm going to be doing a lot of these, so I need to have the basics down. It'll be interesting, like I said, it's patterned more of a Tony Robbins book, so I'm in a dark suit and faded in the background. I did red, because that's our company colors, but it's like the Matrix background behind me, and then it looks very similar to his *Unleashed* book. You'll have to go out and look at the new cover on Amazon.

Sandi: For sure. What advice do you have for other experts who want to publish a book or who are thinking about it or on the fence?

Kevin: I told this financial part of it. I would encourage everybody to do that drill right up front. If you have a bestselling book, what does it mean for what you're offering? What is your average deal size? It becomes a no-brainer at that point. Then if you don't have the skills to do the content and stuff, then exactly like you said, there's folks that you will interview you and transcribe it and clean it up, and then they'll also have professionals that can do the cover.

I did the full nine yards, because it looks like at this point it's such a lucrative thing, and it goes along with if we do a book based around our four areas in our business, and with the tv segments or with our stories that we'll tell at major venues, I think I'm going to end up having at least one or two books a year at this point, going forward. Because you just want to keep that engine going. It's something where you need to pick good people, like yourself, that you know can deliver, and put a marketing plan together. It's not what you're doing today, it's what you've achieved and you're elevating on for next year.

Sandi: The long game. Definitely. Is there anything that you'd like to share or that I should have asked about?

Kevin: The biggest thing is to put your personality in it, and even some quirky background stories about you that are vulnerable.

Sandi: My very last question is what is the website that you would like to me to promote in the book?

Kevin: www.MatrixForce.com

MARYANNE PARKER
– *The Sharpest Soft Skill*

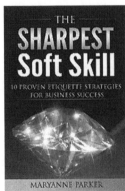
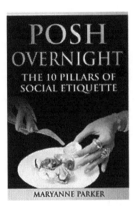

Maryanne is one of my favorite stories. She is truly the embodiment of the American Dream. An immigrant from Bulgaria and a single mom, she picked herself up by the bootstraps, educated herself on etiquette and protocol, earning an executive diploma from the International School of Protocol and Diplomacy in both Brussels and Washington. She founded Manor of Manners, a company that specializes in International Etiquette and Protocol training for adults and children, with an emphasis in business etiquette. Besides all of that, she's involved with Professional Women Group of Dress for Success San Diego, an organization that helps underprivileged women gain financial independence and self-sufficiency. She's a TV personality as well, traveling all over the country (and world) to make appearances on local and national TV. Although I have learned just how uncouth I am through my association with her, she never makes anyone feel bad or embarrassed for not having the proper etiquette, although when asked she's more than happy to share some tips.

Sandi: First of all, I want to ask you about your writing process, that is how you actually went from the idea to the written word.

Maryanne: When I write, because I write training books as a guide, so I have the points written. This makes the process much easier. For example, if I have 10 points to talk about, I develop the first one. When I'm done with the first one, I just move to the second one. This makes everything much more organized.

Sandi: Basically you created an outline, and then took each topic one by one and wrote through it.

Maryanne: Yes. That's exactly true.

Sandi: Was there anything that you found was a challenge in that process? Did you find yourself getting writer's block, or did it all flow pretty smoothly?

Maryanne: It always can be a challenge. I think, for us, if we decide to write something, we have to definitely have a deadline, because if we don't have a dead-line we're going to postpone the process for many months, maybe years. If we decide to write a book, we should do it now. When you start writing, everything becomes a little bit easier, because at least you already started.

Sandi: You get into your flow.

Maryanne: A lot of things can get into the flow, but if we have a deadline it would be much easier, because you know the work has to be done. It's not just a hobby, just sitting at home and writing.

Sandi: Doing the pre-release of the book and having that hard deadline helped you.

Maryanne: Extremely much. Yes. A lot of times I think it's good for a person to have the book written before the pre-release, but if you're not ready, or if you have a lot of things going on, a lot of projects to be completed, the pre-release helps a lot, because the people are aware of what's going on, what is coming in the near future. It structures everything much easier for us, the writers. When I have 90 days, and I have to release it to Amazon, I have no choice but to be done by the deadline.

Sandi: Right. It puts that hard deadline on you that you have to meet.

Maryanne: Yes.

Sandi: That's what helps me as well, doing that. I want to talk a little bit about the before and after. I want to know, before you wrote your first book where you were. I don't mean literally, physically. I don't mean like were you in San Diego or Bulgaria, but I mean with your business, in your life, things like that. What was it that motivated you to want to do the book, and then I also want to know the after. What were the effects of having the book, on your business and your life?

Maryanne: I've seen many people, when they have a book, they become something, they look more sufficient, more efficient, more eligible as not only writers, but as an expert. I always thought maybe I am not the person to write a book, because it's not my first language, or my grammar is not the best, or I don't have the flow of the thought as many other people do. I was writing little blogs here and there, just for my own entertainment. I was writing what I thought might be good for my programs. I decided that this could be a good book. It's not very long. It's very well-structured. I decided to put it together.

Sandi: You would say that one of the effects of having the book was a confidence builder.

Maryanne: Definitely. When you have a book, it's much more impressive for everybody else. If you feel that you're not that important and not so significant, people perceive you on a different scale. You might think that I might write a book, but when you have the book already, obviously you have something to share with the world, especially if you have a good contribution to the community and to the world in general. It's very significant part.

Sandi: I know that you have been doing some amazing awesome things. Can you share with me some of these awesome things that have been happening to you since writing your book?

Maryanne: Having a book has a lot of benefits as well, because a lot of times you can be very well known by people only because you have a book. They don't need to spend time with you, because a lot of people might not be in your location if you held classes or seminars. You can always send them the book. They can purchase it online. You can recommend it. You can send it as a gift. This could be something that you can present to your clients, for free even. It's extremely beneficial.

My second book came because I saw that I want to share more, after the first one. My second book was presented on the Nasdaq Jumbotron. Because of the effect of the book, I don't know if it's the content, but always when you have a book and when you have a second book it becomes even more interesting. People got really fascinated by my business.

139

Sandi: What have you been doing with that notoriety? I know today you had a big win.

Maryanne: Yes. Today I was invited on this show in San Diego, which I sent physically only one of my books, but they saw my other books because it was already on Amazon. They featured both of my books, and they're very impressed, because both of my books are #1 International Best-Sellers. They were interested about the content. I was on the [Big Bus] business show San Diego, and they invited me to be a regular guest for the show. They have another show, which I don't know. I don't remember the name of the show, but there is another one too.

Sandi: That is so awesome. You've been going all over the place doing TV appearances, and now you've been invited to be a regular guest on a business show. That's huge. I'm so excited for you.

Maryanne: Thank you. This is how I formulate my information about me. When I mention I'm the owner of this particular company, but I'm the author of the #1 international best-selling books *The Sharpest Soft Skill* and *Posh Overnight*. This brings a lot of different weight on my persona in general. I think it's very beneficial. I'm so happy that I have the books.

Sandi: What effect has having the book made on your relationships with your competitors, with your industry, and not just with your clients?

Maryanne: You don't want to compete in business, because everybody has their own niche. At the same time, why not dominate your industry? Maybe you have a particular niche, but at the same time you can also dominate. Having only one book, it is a good thing, but you need to be consistent. You have to have at least two or three is what I believe, because probably you have much more content that you'd like to share. I think that has been amazing.

Sandi: You don't like the term "competitors." Let's say "colleagues." The colleagues in your industry, have you noticed a difference in your relationships with them since publishing?

Maryanne: Yes. Definitely. They want to work with you. They want to associate with you. They want to exchange ideas with you. That has been amazing too.

Sandi: You really fashioned yourself to being recognized as an industry thought leader.

Maryanne: We have to be. I don't believe in competition, but I believe in dominance.

Sandi: I love it. We touched on this a little bit earlier, but let's go back to this. What was the hardest part for you of the writing and publishing process?

Maryanne: The hardest part was because I had no idea how this can be done. I always see people having books with those beautiful covers. Everything is written. Everything is so well formatted. I never knew. I felt very intimidated about the process, because I wasn't aware. Now, because I know the process, I know that I can do it.

Sandi: It was kind of being overwhelmed by what you didn't know.

Maryanne: Yes. I didn't know. I'm hearing from a lot of people, I'm not a writer. I don't know how to do this. If I can write a book, and this is not even my first language, not the best grammar in the world, and I'm using my own pictures, which are not even that sufficient, and I have a book on the Nasdaq Jumbotron. Not everybody can do it too.

Sandi: Very nice. You've just done amazing things. I'm in awe of you. What advice do you have for other experts who want to publish a book?

Maryanne: They just have to do it. Right now. Right away. Don't postpone for a minute. There's so many editors out there. There are people who can help you with the process. I think what you do makes everything so much easier, because you introduce the person to the steps. You're so efficient and just very helpful. I think nobody can have an excuse not to write a book, especially when we have the tools now. We know what's going on.

Sandi: Nice. Is there anything else you'd like to share that I didn't ask and should have, or that you'd like to have as part of our conversation?

Maryanne: I'm actually thinking about my next book already. No, not that I'm thinking about anything right now. This is what I think, the books change our life, and it's part of the process. We just have to fit the particular model of an entrepreneur for us to be able to break it, because, first of all, you have to fit in to be able to stand out eventually. You have to have a book. When you have more than one, and you have a #1 international best-seller, we want to go internationally. We don't want to be local, because it's a global environment. It's a global market. As they say, the sky is the limit.

Sandi: Totally. Tell me about a couple of your other wins. I know you were brought to Dubai to speak there. You've done some other pretty amazing things. Maybe just share a couple of those other things real quick.

Maryanne: I shared my book with the Protocol School of Washington. I was very happy, because more of the people were in my class. They got a book from me. I felt so powerful, because in a way I was so happy, because they are already established in their industries. They work for amazing corporations. It's just a very high standard environment, and for me to be known that I have a book and I presented myself in this way, and I had something for them, was really great. I studied in London last year as well for etiquette, because I want to know as much as I can about the industry.

Sandi: Nice. Last question. What is the website that you want me to promote in my book?

Maryanne: www.ManorofManners.com .

BARRY FRIEDMAN
– *I Love Me More Than Sugar*

B arry Friedman was one of my early clients with his book *I Love Me More Than Sugar*. He's a former juggler and a business coach, and all around a pretty amazing guy. He has made a lot of TV appearances talking about living a sugar-free lifestyle. He is someone who I find really inspiring and I always find that whatever he's talking about on social media is just what I need to hear at the moment. I was really excited that he was able to carve some time from his busy schedule to speak with me about his book, and the writing process.

Sandi: what was your writing process? How did you go from the idea of the book to actually having a manuscript?

Barry: There are a couple different styles of work style. I'm very much an agile workstyle person. I like to get an idea as quickly as I can, get a proof of concept, see if it makes any sense. I had been sugar-free for about a year and a half, and I was told by someone we both know that I should write a book. I did what any agile workstyle person would do. I sat down and wrote the table of contents and passed it around to some friends. They said, "I'd read this." Once I had the table of contents, I just cranked out the chapters.

Then I hired a good editor, and I kept sending stuff back and forth with her. Things would come back with marks all over it, and I'd be depressed for three or four days. I'd put it away, and then I'd open it up again, and I'd make some changes and tighten up areas. I went through it. Really, for me, writing the table of contents was huge. Then I just basically had to fill it in.

Sandi: Basically the table of contents acted as an outline, and then you took each chapter and wrote through it.

Barry: Yup. The TOC was my GOD. Yes.

Sandi: What has been the effect of having a book, on your business, in your life? What opportunities have opened up to you because of the book?

Barry: That's a good question. For one thing, I was able to talk--I wrote a book as a loss leader. I never thought I'd make any money on it. Honestly, to this day, I sell at least 100 copies a month on slow months through Amazon, so I get a report every week, and then a monthly ending report. What do I get? It's not a lot of money. I think I get about $3.70 per book, or something.

That's in the background. That just kind of happens. The bigger thing is most of the people who buy the book end up coming to my website, getting on my lists, growing my email list. Some percentage of them become members of my online program. Some members of those programs upsell to my group coaching or my private coaching.

That book was a big opener. I wrote it at a time when I was doing a course on being on TV to get more attention to my product. Having the book allowed me to get on 25 TV shows. That was enough. I didn't want to make a career out of being on local TV and flying around the country. What I wanted was a book to get on TV, and TV so that I could have authority to run my programs online.

Then running my programs online gave me the authority to do upsells and coaching programs and group coaching programs and build a big mailing list, which is a valuable asset. I read about a book, or I hear about a product, or there's a big summit that I can be a part of, having a mailing list is good. I can let people on my list know things that will help them, and if those things sell, sometimes I get a commission from them. Be hard to put a dollar number on the book, but I know it's in the six figures.

Sandi: Have you also used it as leverage for speaking gigs?

Barry: I never did public speaking. I've been on virtual summits. I've been on more of those than I can count, and that's because I wrote the book, and that, again, drives traffic back to my mailing list. I was on the road for 34 years as a professional juggler, and the thought of going out on stages again and doing that all again, I don't have that in me anymore. At this point in my life, I measure my success by the number of days I'm home.

Sandi: I hear you.

Barry: I would definitely say people could do that, if they wrote a book.

Sandi: I think that virtual summits are just as valid as live events, especially in today's world. I would consider that an equal speaking engagement, personally.

Barry: Bigger audience, less hassle. Virtual events are huge now, and you'd never get 25,000, 50,000 people into a room, but they can hear you on a virtual summit.

Sandi: Yes. In other words, yes. It's led you to other opportunities.

Barry: Definitely. I've done a lot of speaking. I got to be on the biggest podcast. I was on a couple big ones. I was on *Entrepreneur on Fire* with John Lee Dumas. I was on *Fat-Burning Man* with Abel James. These are stages. Think of those as speaking appearances. Those are good stages to be on, and I wouldn't have been on either of those had I not written a book. Absolutely.

Sandi: Those are huge stages, for sure. What was the hardest part of the writing and publishing process?

Barry: I think for me it was the actual writing of the book. I had a great editor, who just would not let me slide, would not let me slip, accepted my time schedule. This editor was discerning; that's what I learned from working with this editor, discernment was incredible. Here's what matters. Here's your story. Here's what matters to you. Here's what matters to the book. That was big. That discernment piece was very big for me, and I think I got good at that. I've written a lot of content for my program, for my blogs. Content gets generated nowadays, and what's stayed with me since finishing the book right in the beginning of 2015 was that discernment. What do I feel like I need to get out to tell the story, and what can I leave behind? The more valuable the content is, the less filler, the more it will be read and consumed.

Sandi: Right. Kind of that *War and Peace* thing. He didn't have time to make it a shorter book.

Barry: Exactly. That's the best analogy ever.

Sandi: What advice do you have for other experts who want to publish a book?

Barry: Do it! I'd say there's going to be a lot of demons, a lot of skeletons that come up to kind of get in your way. There's a thing I write about extensively in the sugar-free book about the lizard brain, this part of our brain that more than anything wants to keep us exactly where we are. That lizard brain creates some beautiful excuses. I don't have the right lighting. I don't know when to start. I'm waiting for this one thing to finish. Someone said they'd call me back. Any excuse is the gold for the lizard brain.

Walk over all that. Be clear on what you want. Set small, tangible goals every single day. Make those the very first thing you do in the morning. If you get your stuff done early in the morning, the rest of the day you may even do more, but no matter what you're going to go to bed feeling confident. You're going to feel accomplished. Waiting till later in the day, again, that's the land of the lizard brain, waiting till later in the day. Land of the Lizard.

Sandi: I like that. I know on balloon jobs I hate getting up for the 0-dark-thirty jobs, but when it's 6:00 a.m., and I've already made my money for the day, I feel great.

Barry: I swim with a master's swim club here. We swim across this lake three mornings a week. The sun's down. The boats haven't come out on the water yet. The moon is setting, and we finish at 6:45 a.m. I go, "I don't care if I sit on the couch and eat cookies the rest of the day," which I don't do. It's good. The earlier you can get yourself feeling like I've accomplished, who knows? You may have another spurt later in the day, and that's a double win.

Sandi: I love that. That's great advice. My last question.

Barry: It's going to be a hard one.

Sandi: It is. It's the hardest one. Is there anything else you'd like to share? Is there anything that I should have asked?

Barry: In a book for helping people write books, I've probably already iterated enough, don't be your own editor.

Sandi: Bring on a team to help you with the technical stuff.

Barry: My gosh, just don't be your own editor. Don't be the final person to say this book is ready. Get it read by an outside eye. Not your spouse, but someone you're actually paying, who has editing credits and is an editor, because that set of eyes, that feedback, will be invaluable to you, to your book being readable, versus something that's readable to you. We have this thing, I turn something in, and I think it's perfect, or I wouldn't have written it. The truth is, someone who knows the book market, knows what an actual book should look like, the shape and form of it, they can instantly see this is not part of the book. That's a gift. That's a huge gift. It's not expensive to have a good editor. If you're looking to have a book that's readable and will drive traffic or eyeballs or followers to your movement, it's worth spending whatever, $750-$1,000, to get someone to edit your book. If it's not worth that, you may not have a business.

Sandi: last question, which I need to include in here, is what is the website that you want me to point to in the book?

Barry: http://www.30dayssugarfree.com

DR. TAMIKA ANDERSON
– *Speak Up and Get Out!*

 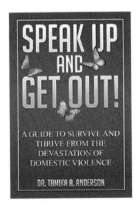 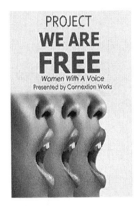

Dr. Tamika Anderson, founder of the Speak Up, Speak Out Movement, helps women who have survived domestic violence find their voice, strength, and help getting out of an abusive situation. Dr. Tamika knows from both personal experience and from experience in the trenches the trauma that these women face. A survivor herself, she has built an incredible career out of helping other women and being a light for them. At the time of this writing she is a two-time best-selling author, with a third book on the way.

Sandi: I just want to ask you a few questions about your books. You have written two books and have a third in the works. What are the titles?

Tamika: My first book is called *Speak Up and Get Out: How to Survive and Thrive After the Devastation of Domestic Violence.* The second book is *Project We Are Free: Women With a Voice.*

Sandi: Awesome. These are both important books. You have a really big message that you want to share and get out there. Please share a couple of words about your message and your mission, and then we'll talk more specifically about your books.

Tamika: Okay. My message is two-fold. I help women know the red flags of domestic violence and how to escape potentially deadly situations, and then once they get through that phase, there's another group of women that I help find their voice, tell their story, and take the stage. It doesn't necessarily mean literally taking the stage, which some of us do. Some of the women do, and we'll get into that with *Project We Are Free.* It's just a matter of taking the stage of your life, because sometimes our voice has been muted, and we don't even realize it. Our power has been stripped from us, and we don't even realize that our power has been stripped. For some of us, we don't even realize that we had the power to begin with.

Sandi: I think that's a common problem for women, even if they haven't been in overtly abusive relationships, just knowing our worth and knowing that we're allowed to have a voice.

Tamika: That is correct. A lot of times people think that abuse is physical, but it is not only physical. It is verbal, emotional, financial, sexual, which is a form of physical abuse. It can be all of those different things. It's not always done in a mean, hostile manner. It can sometimes, as I say, be served up with a hug and a smile. There are a lot of women who are out here that are being abused, and they don't even know it.

Sandi: With your second book, *Project We Are Free*, you started bringing in other women to talk about their experiences. Tell me more about that book.

Tamika: *Speak Up and Get Out* was such a hit, I guess you can say. It's not a record, but it was a hit, because there were so many women talking about it. Even a woman who had spent 30 years at a shelter, working for the shelter, told me that she uses that book as like a Bible. So many women heard about the *Speak Up, Speak Out* movement that when I presented *Project We Are Free* it was to be able to give other women a platform to share their story.

What I did is I opened up a few slots. There was a total of eight women. Each woman wrote a chapter in the book to share her story. Then each woman took the stage to share her story in front of a live audience. It was so powerful. It was moving. One woman in the audience said that she was so glad that we had written the book, and glad that we had the live event, because it gave her permission to give her daughter permission to have a voice. There were men in the audience, grown men, who were shedding tears and who felt the need to finally open up about different things that they had experienced in life. We're going to open up the book to men.

Sandi: Wow. Your movement is really affecting generations. This is pretty incredible. This is important work that you're doing.

Tamika: Yes. Generations, for sure. Some of the women who had done a chapter in the book said because of *Project We Are Free*, I am able to mend the relationship with my mother that had been broken. There have been relationships that have been mended. There has been a lot of healing that has taken place, from just open wounds, wounds that had been unhealed over the years. They're getting rid of the toxic mindset and the toxic feelings and crushing the fears.

Sandi: Incredible. Let's talk a little bit about your writing process. What was your process? How did you go from the idea to actually the written word?

Tamika: For *Speak Up and Get Out,* what I did is I was in a situation where I couldn't believe that I was the woman who had been abused and who had to escape abuse. I felt like if I was being abused, and I didn't know it, how many women are out there who are in this same position, and how many women out there know they're being abused, but they're just afraid to speak up, because of the victim blaming and shaming? What I did is I basically just told my story of how and when I met my abuser, and then I just took them on a journey to present day.

Sandi: Did you go straight to paper, or did you perform it or speak it first? Did you do an outline?

Tamika: I did an outline. What I did is I took a great big sticky note, and then from there I took smaller sticky notes and posted them onto the big sticky note just to have somewhat of an outline, because I didn't want to just tell my story from this woe is me place. I wanted to tell the story from here is the bad part, here is how it starts out, and just take them through the process, but then I also did it in a way where they could actually journal in the book. It's somewhat of a workbook where they could work through their feelings and different things that they could do in order to be kind to themselves as they go through the process of healing. It's somewhat of a workbook as well. I want women to be able to tell their story and not get stuck in their story. I want us to be able to share our story from a place of courage and empowerment.

Sandi: Obviously you know your story. You didn't have to figure out how to tell your story necessarily. You brainstormed with your sticky notes, figuring the points you wanted to make and the tips and hints that you wanted to give.

Tamika: Yes. I did the brainstorm, and I used the sticky notes so that I could move them around if I needed to and place them in a different order if I needed to. It was the brainstorm, then it was the outline, and then from the outline I just went through each one and began to build the chapters.

Sandi: Then went back through the editing to find where it needed more information.

Tamika: Yes. Then you go back through, and you look and say, this section needs more information, or you go back through and say, I need to be a little more detailed here. You go back through and just see where you may have missed something or where something may have been unclear. Then go back through again just to make sure that the order flows the way you want it to flow, and that your message is coming across as clearly as possible.

Sandi: For the second book, *Project We Are Free*, you had other people contributing chapters. What was that process like? Did you have a process that you were leading them through to help them get their words out to paper? Did you just give them a deadline and say submit it? How did that kind of all come together?

Tamika: I gave them different pointers on different writing styles that they could do, but because most of us, and most of the women that I work with, have been controlled and have not had the opportunity to make decisions for themselves, what I did is I told them this is your story. I want you to be able to share your story in a way that it comes across clear and concise, and people get it, the only condition was, just don't use anyone's name or the name of a business. Of course, we don't want to get sued, right?

I wanted them to feel free to express themselves, because so often, you may have heard this saying, what goes on in this house stays in this house, and you don't air our dirty laundry. Right? I wanted them to be able to say this is my moment to unpack my bags of anger, of frustration, of guilt, grudges, resentment, fear, rejection. I wanted them to let it all go.

The beautiful part about it, Sandi, is that when they ended up taking the stage their styles were so unique and different. Some of them did it in poetry form. Some of them just told their stories off

161

the top of their head. Others did a little song before they went into their story, but the song was a part of the story. It was just phenomenal.

Sandi: Did any of them get overwhelmed by trying to get their thoughts to paper or anything like that?

Tamika: I would say initially yes, but once we started doing the one-on-one coaching calls, it took away all the anxiety that they had around it. Oftentimes we have a fear of the unknown, so at that time they didn't know what to expect. As we did the one-on-one coaching calls, we peeled back the onion layers to get to the core of what their actual story was, and then built around the one major moment in their life where they may have experienced some trauma or shift or some exciting moment.

Sandi: Having you to talk it out with helped them clarify what they were trying to say,

Tamika: Yes. By the time they were going to get on stage, I even told them, if you are so nervous that you need for me to get on stage and stand behind you, because I've got your back, I'd be willing to do that. It turned out each woman got up there in such a courageous manner, and they spoke their truth. Before they even got on stage, as I said before, we did the one-on-one. Then we did it as a group, because I wanted them to have an audience. Even though it was online, via video chat, they still had an audience. By the time they got on stage, they were ready. Yet, it still had the authenticity and transparency to move the audience. We all ended up still in tears, even though we'd heard the stories. Even the night before, I had them do a run through, a dry run, to go through it.

Sandi: What has come about as a result of having published your books?

Tamika: Since I've published my books, *Speak Up and Get Out* has been on television numerous times on some major networks, NBC, ABC, Fox, Radio One. I've been on some major networks. Then I've been able to collaborate with celebrities. I've shared the stage with a Grammy nominated singer as a result. A lot of people find me online as a result of my book. I just believe that the book has saved lives. I receive messages from people who tell me that my book has saved their life or changed their life. Those are some of the things that the book has done.

Sandi: That has got to feel so good, when somebody comes up to you and says, your book saved my life. That's just got to feel great when you know that you had that kind of impact.

Tamika: Yeah. Every single time it feels like the first time that I've heard it, because that's something that I don't take lightly.

163

Sandi: For the other women who collaborated with you for *Project We Are Free*, have you heard anything back from them on changes in their life or the effect?

Tamika: Yes. The women, what I've heard back from them, they're now using the title published author, because they're now published authors. They've also told me that they are now able to get into venues that they otherwise would not have been able to get into, had it not been for *Project We Are Free*. They are now collaborating with people who they otherwise would not have been able to be connected with, had it not been for *Project We Are Free*.

A few women have some book signings coming up. One woman has a celebrity book signing coming up. There's going to be celebrities there, and she's going to be doing a book signing with celebrities there around the *Project We Are Free* book. She's going to be in Hollywood, in LA. We're all excited about that, because it's really taking off. It has really taken off to a place that I just didn't see coming.

Sandi: That's true. Once you start going, things just happen on their own volition, and amazing things happen that you could never have predicted beforehand.

Tamika: Right. Things you just couldn't imagine.

Sandi: What was the hardest part, or the biggest challenge, of the writing/publishing process for you?

Tamika: I don't have any. I really don't. I think because I was so laser focused on helping somebody else, like I've got to get this out there, that I just didn't have any challenges. There were some parts where it was a little emotional for me. It was emotional for me to write it, because it tapped into a pain that I didn't want to revisit, but because I knew that I needed to get the book out there I didn't have that writer's block.

Sandi: You had a really solid team around you as well.

Tamika: Yeah.

Sandi: I think that can definitely help make the process much smoother, the actual physical process of it.

Tamika: When it came to actually getting the book published and on the public platform, I must say you and your team were brilliant.

Sandi: Thank you. I wasn't fishing, but I do appreciate it.

Tamika: Super smooth. Honestly, because that would be considered a part of the publishing side of it. Right. When it comes to that, I didn't have any issues, because you walked me through it step by step, kept me in the loop of the process. No. I didn't have any issues, because you and your team were just phenomenal.

Sandi: Thank you. Appreciate it. What advice do you have for other experts who want to publish a book?

Tamika: I'd say don't delay. Do not delay. There's somebody out there who needs your story. They need to read the words that you have written in your book. I know that you said that your books are fluff, but you'd be surprised at the lives that you have impacted and changed as a result of your books. There could be somebody out there who is so down and dejected, and they found a new way of life through your books of the balloons.

Sandi: That is a good point. We never know the impact that we're going to have on people. Just recently, when I was teaching at a convention, at a balloon convention, people were coming up to me and telling me, I started my business because of you. You're right. You never know. Once you put it out there into the world, you have no idea the impact that it's going to have, even if it's something like a balloon recipe book.

Tamika: Exactly. Look at it this way, if someone is telling you that your balloon book started their business, being able to build a business around that is actually saving someone financially too.

Sandi: Right.

Tamika: We know that financial burdens can sometimes lead to suicide. You've saved a life there, when you look at it in that perspective. Unfortunately, I deal a lot with people who have dealt with murder/ suicide. One of the top things is finances. Finances will sometimes contribute to domestic violence and abuse. It's about power and control.

Sandi: Right. I think it's beneficial any time somebody can find something that can give them hope that the world can look differently.

Tamika: Yes.

Sandi: Last question, is there anything else you'd like to share, or anything that I forgot to ask?

Tamika: Your services are top notch. Anyone who needs to have their book published should utilize your services.

Sandi: I appreciate that. Thank you.

Tamika: I don't know if that's what you're looking for or not. You can put it into your own words, but I don't endorse people like that, because I know the good when I see it and experience it, and I know the bad when I see it and experience it. You've been really good to me.

Sandi: You're very kind. Thank you. Is there anything I forgot to ask, or do you want to share?

Tamika: I can't think of anything else.

Sandi: What website can people go to for more information about you and Project We Are Free?

Tamika: www.TamikaAnderson.com and they can also join our free supportive community at www.SpeakUpSpeakOutNetwork.com

CONCLUSION

There's really nothing like the feeling of holding your book for the first time! I'm really excited for you to be on this journey!

As you've learned from the authors I interviewed, the most important thing is just getting started. Just do it. To save yourself frustration, get a good team behind you, and then just go for it!

I've prepared a cheat sheet/ checklist for you, which you can download at www.ExpertBook4U.com/checklist .

I'd love to help you turn your dream into a reality, so if you'd like to schedule a 15 minute consultation with me to talk about your book, you can do so here,

www.ExpertBook4U.com/Appointment

Also, come join my Facebook group where you can get your questions answered, network with other aspiring authors, get helpful tips and resources and hang out with some cool people, www.Facebook.com/groups/SandisBookClub

I'm looking forward to seeing you in the group or meeting with you. And most importantly, I can't wait to read your book!!!

Now, go forth and bookify!!!!!

ABOUT THE AUTHOR

Sandi Masori wears many hats. She has helped over 100 authors publish their business authority books, and has appeared on TV more than 90 times. Recently she sold her balloon business, but still maintains her YouTube channel and her book series *The DIY Balloon Bible*. Currently she is working on producing a new show called *Shape Up Sandi*, which is a light-hearted, fish-out-of-water transformational journey featuring segments on fitness activities, healthy lifestyle, cooking, beauty/ style, and mindset/ motivation. While she is passionate about helping authors self-publish, she feels that her most important hat is that of "mom."

49739854R00100

Made in the USA
Columbia, SC
27 January 2019